J286   Book   6.50
J287   Compact Disc   10.00
J288   Book & CD   16.50

**PERCUSSION
REVISED EDITION**

Richard F. Grunow
*Professor of Music Education
Eastman School of Music
of the University of Rochester*

Edwin E. Gordon
*Research Professor
University of South Carolina*

Christopher D. Azzara
*Associate Professor of Music Education
Eastman School of Music
of the University of Rochester*

STUDENT BOOK ONE

AN INSTRUMENTAL METHOD DESIGNED FOR DEVELOPING AUDIATION SKILLS AND EXECUTIVE SKILLS

Instrument	Bk 1	CD 1	Bk1 & CD	Bk 2	CD 2	Bk2 & CD	Solo Bk 1A w. CD	Solo Bk 1B w. CD	Solo Bk 2	Solo Bk 3
Flute	J250	J251	J252	J289		J290	J339	J353	J150	J204
Clarinet	J253	J254	J255	J291		J292	J340	J354	J151	J205
Oboe	J256	J257	J258	J293		J294	J341	J355	J152	J206
Bassoon	J259	J260	J261	J295		J296	J342	J356	J153	J207
Alto Sax	J262	J263	J264	J297		J298	J343	J357	J154	J208
Tenor Sax	J265	J266	J267	J299		J300	J344	J358	J155	J209
Trumpet	J268	J269	J270	J301		J302	J345	J359	J156	J210
Horn in F	J271	J272	J273	J303		J304	J346	J360	J157	J211
Trombone	J274	J275	J276	J305		J306	J347	J361	J158	J212
Baritone BC	J277	J278	J279	J307		J308	J348	J362	J159	J213
Baritone TC	J280	J281	J282	J309		J310	J349	J363	J160	J214
Tuba	J283	J284	J285	J311	J316	J312	J350	J364	J161	J215
Percussion	J286	J287	J288	J313		J314	J351	J365	J162	J216
Recorder	J231	J232	J233	J247	J245CD	J245	J94		J149	J217

Revised Teacher Guide for Band Books 1 and 2	J315
Solo Book 1–Writing (all instruments)	J167
Solo Book 2–Writing (all instruments)	J168
Solo Book 3–Writing (all instruments)	J203
Composition Book 1 (all instruments)	J249
Revised Teacher's Guide for Recorder	J235
GIA Heavy Duty Sporano Recorder	M447
JRI for Strings (specify instrument)	

Concert Selections

Full score (all twelve works) J178
Flute (J179) • Oboe (J180) • Clarinet I (J181) • Clarinet II (J182) • Bass Clarinet (J183) • Bassoon (J184) • Alto Saxophone (J185) • Tenor Saxophone (J186) • Baritone Saxophone (J187) • Trumpet I (J188) • Trumpet II (J189) • Horn (J190) • Trombone I (J191) • Trombone II (J192) • Baritone B.C. (J193) • Baritone T.C. (J194) • Tuba (J195) • Bells/Xylophone/Piano (J196) • Percussion (J197)
Demonstration compact disc J198CD

Recorded Solos with Accompaniments

Cassette Bk 1A & 1B :	Cassette Bk 2:	Cassette Bk 3:
J99	J148	J200
CD Bk 1:	CD Bk 2:	CD Bk 3:
J99CD	J148CD	J200CD

Listening

Simple Gifts	*Don Gato*	*You Are My Sunshine*
Cassette:	Cassette:	Cassette:
J229CS	J201CS	J199CS
CD:	CD:	CD:
J229CD	J201CD	J199CD

GIA Publications, Inc., 7404 S. Mason Ave., Chicago, IL 60638

2

ASSIGNMENT SCHEDULE

The teacher will specify the student's assignments. The student will insert the date and check (✓) underneath the date to indicate specific assignments. The *Home-Study Compact Disc* Track # is the same as the Item Number.

READ THE FOLLOWING	Page No.	DATE	DATE	DATE	DATE	DATE	DATE	DATE	DATE	DATE	DATE	DATE	DATE	DATE	DATE	DATE	DATE
A NOTE TO PARENTS AND STUDENTS	ii																
PRACTICE TIPS	4																
USE OF THE *HOME-STUDY COMPACT DISC*	5																
PLAYING IN TUNE WITH THE *HOME-STUDY COMPACT DISC*	5																
RIGHT HAND AND LEFT HAND POSITION-MATCHED GRIP	5																
THE STROKE - BEATING SPOT AND POSITION - STICKING GUIDELINES	6																
PERFORMING ON THE MALLET (KEYBOARD) PERCUSSION BELLS AND GLOCKENSPIEL	6																
XYLOPHONE AND MARIMBA	7																
PERFORMING ON THE BASS DRUM - PERFORMING ON THE CYMBALS	7																
ORGANIZING THE PERCUSSION SECTION	7																
MUSICAL ENRICHMENT	47																

LISTEN TO THE HOME-STUDY COMPACT DISC AND FOLLOW THE DIRECTIONS FOR

Item/Track No.	Unit	DATE	DATE	DATE	DATE	DATE	DATE	DATE	DATE	DATE	DATE	DATE	DATE	DATE	DATE	DATE	DATE
1 - Singing "Major Duple" a-Melody b-Bass Line	1-A																
2 - Accompaniment for Singing "Major Duple"																	
3 - Connected Style of Articulation																	
4 - Separated Style of Articulation																	
5 - Singing "Major Triple" a-Melody b-Bass Line	1-B																
6 - Accompaniment for Singing "Major Triple"																	
7 - Connected and Separated Styles of Articulation with the Airstream																	
8 - Connected and Separated Styles of Articulation on the Practice Pad																	
9 - Singing "Minor Duple" a-Melody b-Bass Line	2-A																
10 - Accompaniment for Singing "Minor Duple"																	
11 - Tonal Patterns - Major - Tonic and Dominant - Neutral Syllable																	
12 - Tonal Patterns - Major - Tonic and Dominant - Tonal Syllables																	
13 - Connected and Separated Styles of Articulation on B♭-DO																	
14 - Singing "Minor Triple" a-Melody b-Bass Line	2-B																
15 - Accompaniment for Singing "Minor Triple"																	
16 - Connected and Separated Styles of Articulation on TI																	
17 - Melodic Patterns on B♭-DO and TI																	
18 - Rhythm Patterns - Duple - Macro and Micro - Neutral Syllable																	
19 - Rhythm Patterns - Duple - Macro and Micro - Rhythm Syllables																	
20 - Singing "Pierrot" a-Melody b-Bass Line	3-A																
21 - Accompaniment for Singing "Pierrot"																	
22 - Tonal Patterns - Minor - Tonic and Dominant - Neutral Syllable																	
23 - Tonal Patterns - Minor - Tonic and Dominant - Tonal Syllables																	
24 - Connected and Separated Styles of Articulation on RE																	
25 - Melodic Patterns on B♭-DO, TI and RE																	

Item/Track No.	DATE	DATE	DATE	DATE	DATE	DATE	DATE	DATE	DATE	DATE	DATE	DATE	DATE	DATE	DATE	DATE
26 - Singing "Go Tell Aunt Rhody" a-Melody b-Bass Line 3-B																
27 - Accompaniment for Singing "Go Tell Aunt Rhody"																
28 - Rhythm Patterns - Triple - Macro and Micro - Neutral Syllable																
29 - Rhythm Patterns - Triple - Macro and Micro - Rhythm Syllables																
30 - Connected and Separated Styles of Articulation on MI																
31 - Melodic Patterns on MI and RE																
32 - Melodic Patterns on B♭-DO, TI, RE and MI																
33 - Patterns from "Major Duple" - Connected Style																
34 - Patterns from "Major Duple" - Separated Style																
35 - Performances of "Major Duple" - Connected and Separated Styles																
36 - "Major Duple" - Accompaniments Only																
37 - Singing "Twinkle, Twinkle, Little Star" a-Melody b-Bass Line 4-A																
38 - Accompaniment for Singing "Twinkle, Twinkle, Little Star"																
39 - Patterns from "Major Triple" - Connected Style																
40 - Patterns from "Major Triple" - Separated Style																
41 - Performances of "Major Triple" - Connected and Separated Styles																
42 - "Major Triple" - Accompaniments Only																
43 - Melodic Patterns on E♭-DO and TI																
44 - Singing "Hot Cross Buns" a-Melody b-Bass Line 4-B																
45 - Accompaniment for Singing "Hot Cross Buns"																
46 - Melodic Patterns on E♭-DO, TI, and RE																
47 - Melodic Patterns on MI and RE																
48 - Melodic Patterns on E♭-DO, TI, RE, and MI																
49 - Patterns from "Pierrot"																
50 - Performance of "Pierrot"																
51 - "Pierrot" - Accompaniment Only																
52 - Singing "Lightly Row" a-Melody b-Bass Line 5-A																
53 - Accompaniment for Singing "Lightly Row"																
54 - Melodic Patterns on C-LA and SI																
55 - Melodic Patterns on C-LA, SI, TI, and DO																
56 - Performances of "Minor Duple" - Connected and Separated Styles																
57 - Performances of "Minor Triple" - Connected and Separated Styles																
58 - "Minor Duple" - Accompaniments Only																
59 - "Minor Triple" - Accompaniments Only																
60 - Singing "Down By the Station" a-Melody b-Bass Line 5-B																
61 - Accompaniment for Singing "Down By the Station"																
62 - Rhythm Patterns - Duple - Divisions - Neutral Syllable																
63 - Rhythm Patterns - Duple - Divisions - Rhythm Syllables																
64 - Melodic Patterns on F-DO and SO																
65 - Melodic Patterns on SO and LA																
66 - Melodic Patterns on F-DO, RE, MI, FA, SO, and LA																
67 - Performance of "Twinkle, Twinkle, Little Star"																
68 - "Twinkle, Twinkle, Little Star" - Accompaniment Only																
69 - "Go Tell Aunt Rhody" - Accompaniment Only (F-DO)																

	DATE	DATE	DATE	DATE	DATE	DATE	DATE	DATE	DATE	DATE	DATE	DATE	DATE	DATE	DATE	DATE
70 - Singing "Triple Twinkle" a-Melody b-Bass Line 6-A																
71 - Accompaniment for Singing "Triple Twinkle"																
72 - Tonal Patterns - Major - Tonic, Dominant, Subdominant - Neutral Syllable																
73 - Tonal Patterns - Major - Tonic, Dominant, Subdominant - Tonal Syllables																
74 - Singing "Minor Aunt Rhody" a-Melody b-Bass Line 6-B																
75 - Accompaniment for Singing "Minor Aunt Rhody"																
76 - Rhythm Patterns - Triple - Divisions - Neutral Syllable																
77 - Rhythm Patterns - Triple - Divisions - Rhythm Syllables																
78 - "Lightly Row" - Accompaniment Only (F-DO)																
79 - Singing "Triple Pierrot" a-Melody b-Bass Line 7-A																
80 - Accompaniment for Singing "Triple Pierrot"																
81 - Tonal Patterns - Minor - Tonic, Dominant, Subdominant - Neutral Syllable																
82 - Tonal Patterns - Minor - Tonic, Dominant, Subdominant - Tonal Syllables																
83 - "Down By the Station" - Accompaniment Only (F-DO)																
84 - Singing "Patsy, Ory, Ory, Aye" a-Melody b-Bass Line 7-B																
85 - Accompaniment for Singing "Patsy, Ory, Ory, Aye"																
86 - Rhythm Patterns - Duple - Elongations - Neutral Syllable																
87 - Rhythm Patterns - Duple - Elongations - Rhythm Syllables																
88 - Singing "Baa, Baa, Black Sheep" a-Melody b-Bass Line 8-A																
89 - Accompaniment for Singing "Baa, Baa, Black Sheep"																
90 - Singing "Oats, Peas, Beans" a-Melody b-Bass Line 8-B																
91 - Accompaniment for Singing "Oats, Peas, Beans"																
92 - Rhythm Patterns - Triple - Elongations - Neutral Syllable																
93 - Rhythm Patterns - Triple - Elongations - Rhythm Syllables																
94-97 Musical Enrichment - See page 47.																

PRACTICE TIPS

Under typical circumstances, you should practice every day. When first learning to play an instrument, however, it is most effective if you practice for shorter periods of time. Two sessions of 10 to 15 minutes each day are better than one longer session. Although you will be able to practice for longer periods of time after the first several lessons, it will still be most beneficial if you continue practicing for two shorter sessions, as opposed to one longer session.

How you practice is more important than the length of time you practice. To establish goals for each practice session you should refer to the *Assignment Schedule* on pages 2 - 4, along with the information and illustrations on pages 5 - 7. It is also important to read carefully the guidelines for developing executive skills, which include embouchure, articulation, fingering, posture, and hand position.

USE OF THE HOME-STUDY COMPACT DISC

The *Home-Study Compact Disc* (CD) is an important part of *Jump Right In: The Instrumental Series*. The CD should be played on good equipment. If you do not have a CD player, ask your teacher if you may use one to practice with during the school day, or if you may borrow a CD player from the school or a music store until you obtain your own.

You will use the CD when you practice at home. During your lessons at school, your teacher will explain how to practice at home with your CD. Every item on the CD will be used to help you learn a specific assignment in this book, as explained on the *Assignment Schedule* on pages 2 - 4. For example, after the first lesson you will be asked to listen to the CD and follow the directions for Items 1, 2, 3, and 4. Listen to and follow the directions as many times as you wish. You may replay items on the CD as many times as necessary. Ask your teacher for permission, however, before you listen to items that have not been assigned.

When using the CD, you will typically want to review previous assignments. Perhaps there will be times when you will wish to start with the assignment given in your last lesson. In that case, simply call up the number of that item on the CD player. If you have the "repeat" option on your CD player, you may use it to repeat the item as many times as you wish.

Ask your teacher for help if you are having a problem with following the directions for *Use of the Home-Study Compact Disc*. Protect your CD when you are not practicing by storing it in the plastic sleeve included in this book.

PLAYING IN TUNE WITH THE HOME-STUDY COMPACT DISC

Because the speed of compact disc players is generally consistent, you should be able to play in tune with the compact disc. In addition to performing on your instrument, you will benefit by listening to the compact disc and by singing the songs, chanting the rhythm patterns, and singing the tonal patterns. Except when playing with the accompaniments that are provided on the compact disc, you should ALWAYS REPEAT on your instrument AFTER you hear the musical example on the compact disc. DO NOT PERFORM on your instrument WITH what you are hearing on the compact disc.

RIGHT HAND AND LEFT HAND POSITION - MATCHED GRIP

A matched grip is recommended for the drum pad, snare drum, and all keyboard percussion instruments. When using the matched grip, the position for both hands is the same. The stick is held between the first joint of the index finger and the thumb, about 1/3 of the distance from the end of the stick. The thumb should rest flat on the stick with the index finger slightly curled along the opposite side. This forms a pivot point. The stick motion is controlled from the pivot point. The other three fingers curl around the stick and rest lightly on the back of the stick. The stick lies diagonally across the palm with the palm facing the floor when performing on the instrument. See Figures 1, 2, and 3.

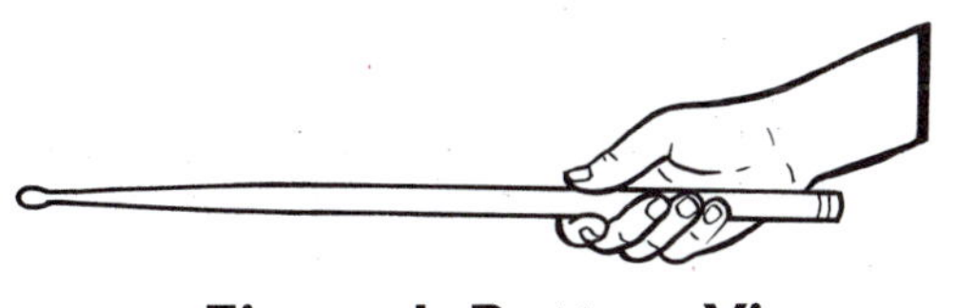

Figure 1. Bottom View

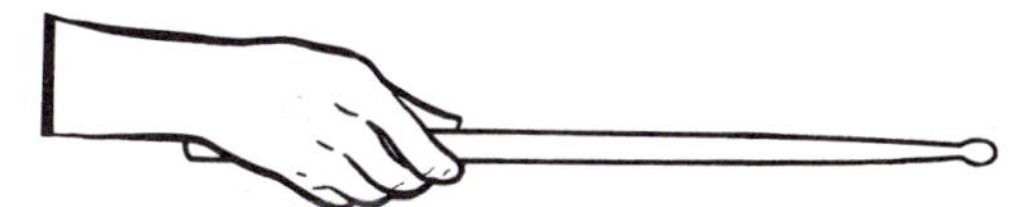

Figure 2. Top View

THE STROKE

The stroke is primarily a wrist motion moving the tip of the stick straight up and down. The arms should be held comfortably at the side. A single stroke motion is similar to waving the hand up and down. The wrist moves the stick down to strike the drum. Then, with a lifting motion, it follows the natural rebound of the stroke back up to the starting position. Think of "pulling" the sound OUT of the instrument. See Figure 3.

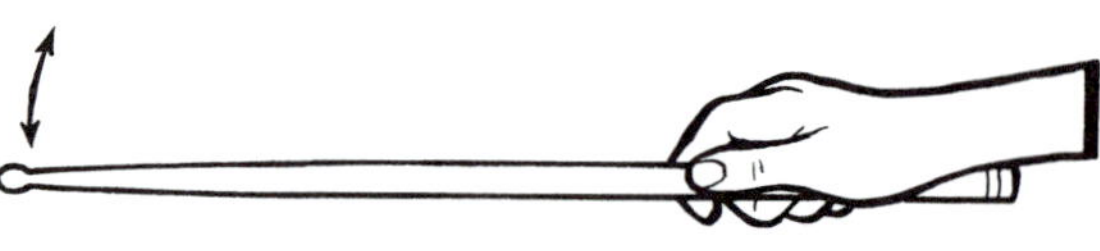

Figure 3.

BEATING SPOT AND POSITION

To obtain the best sound, play directly over the snare bed 1/3 the distance from the rim to the center. The sticks should be held at about a 70 degree angle to each other. The playing surface should be approximately at waist level. The player should stand erect with his or her weight evenly distributed on both feet. See Figures 4, 5, and 6.

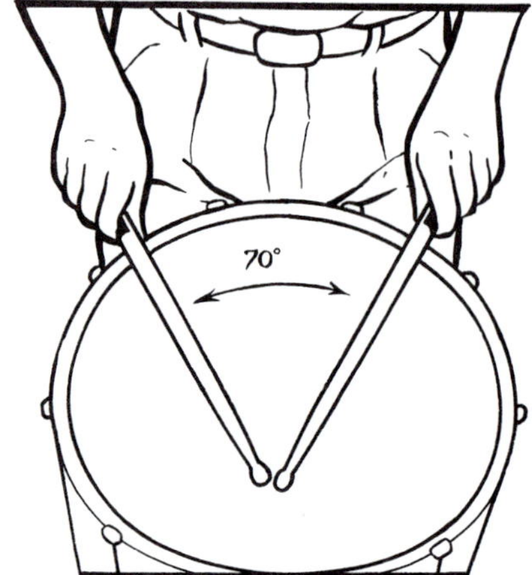

Figure 4.

STICKING GUIDELINES

For the keyboard instruments, always use alternating sticking. Begin with the specified hand (R=right, L=left) except where exceptions have been indicated.

When performing on a practice pad or snare drum, echo the rhythm patterns beginning with the right hand and then echo the same rhythm patterns beginning with the left hand. Continue echoing each pattern with alternate sticking.

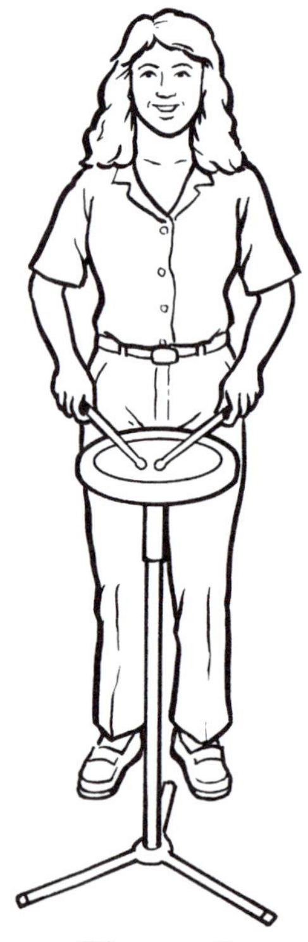

Figure 5.

Figure 6.

PERFORMING ON THE MALLET (KEYBOARD) PERCUSSION INSTRUMENTS

BELLS AND GLOCKENSPIEL

The bars or keys on the bells are made of steel or aluminum. They are arranged in the same pattern as the piano keyboard. The mallets used to play the bells are hard plastic. Rubber or brass mallets can be used to obtain different sounds. The hand position used on the mallets is similar to the snare drum grip. Keep the mallets controlled in the hand, but do not create tension by squeezing the mallets too tightly. The stroke is made with the wrist which moves straight up and down to strike the center of the bar. The mallets should be held at approximately a 90 degree angle to facilitate movement up and down on the keyboard. The playing surface should be at waist level.

XYLOPHONE AND MARIMBA

The xylophone and marimba are keyboard percussion instruments made of wooden bars. The xylophone bars are thick and require the use of hard plastic or rubber mallets. Marimba bars are thinner and should not be struck with hard plastic mallets. Soft rubber or yarn covered mallets are preferred. To sustain a pitch on the xylophone and marimba, a fast succession of single strokes on the same pitch, called a "roll," will lengthen the sound.

PERFORMING ON THE BASS DRUM

The low sound of the bass drum forms the foundation for the concert percussion section. Proper stroke, beating spot, and beater choice should be taken into account when choosing the appropriate sound. 1) Stroke - Using the forearm and wrist, the striking motion is a direct stroke into the head, not a glancing blow. For more forceful volume, the motion should begin from the shoulder. 2) Beating spot - There are three main beating spots for different effects: a) near the edge - soft, light playing; b) approximately 1/3 of the distance from the rim to the center - general playing; and c) close to the center - articulate, dry playing. 3) Beaters - A general purpose beater should be large enough to draw out the full tone of the bass drum and it should have a soft, yet firm surface. A slightly smaller, matched pair of beaters should be used for rolls or rhythm passages. Muffling the bass drum at the end of a sound should be done with the right hand on the beating head and with the left hand on the resonating head.

PERFORMING ON THE CYMBALS

Cymbals are often played in unison with the bass drum, although single cymbal crashes are common. To grip the cymbals, place the strap across the palm, touching the second joint of the index finger to the bell of the cymbal. Curl the remaining fingers around the back of the strap to keep the index finger firmly on the cymbal. Place the flat of the thumb on top of the strap to help control the cymbal motion. For a single crash, place the cymbals in the starting position, dropping the right cymbal as the left cymbal rises to make the cymbals contact each other. At the moment of impact the wrists should be loose, allowing the cymblas to ring freely as they are suspended from the hands. Dampen the cymbals by placing them against your chest or upper arms. For shorter, successive crashes hold the cymbals more vertically, and make a more direct in and out motion.

ORGANIZING THE PERCUSSION SECTION

Organizing the percussion section requires attention to the size of the ensemble and to the instruments needed. The five main areas of the concert percussion section are named below and pictured on the back of the percussion book: 1) Mallet Instruments, 2) Snare Drum, 3) Cymbals, 4) Bass Drum, and 5) Timpani. A typical arrangement should have the timpani positioned beside the bass drum, and preferably near the bass or tuba section of the ensemble. The bass drummer and cymbal player often have similar parts to play and should be located close together and close to the center of the ensemble. The snare drum and accessory instruments should be next in line with the mallet instruments at the end. The arrangement will vary, depending on the number of instruments required to perform a given piece of music. It requires specific skills to play each instrument in the percussion section. Players should rotate positions to learn each skill.

KEYBOARD ORGANIZATION

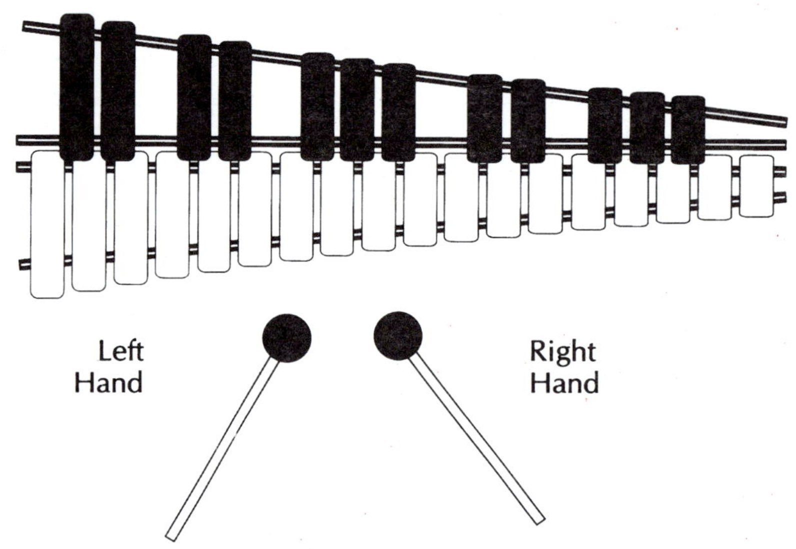

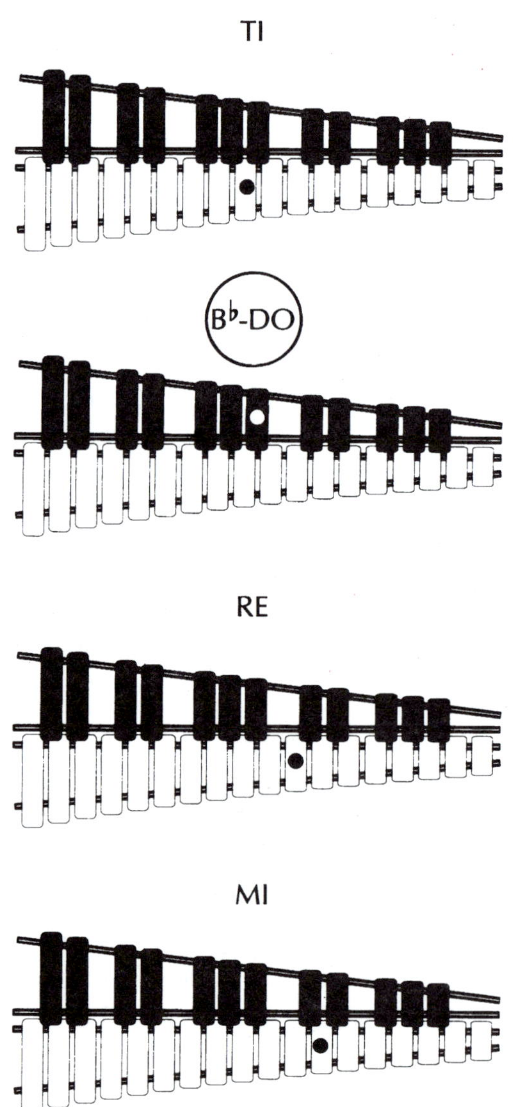

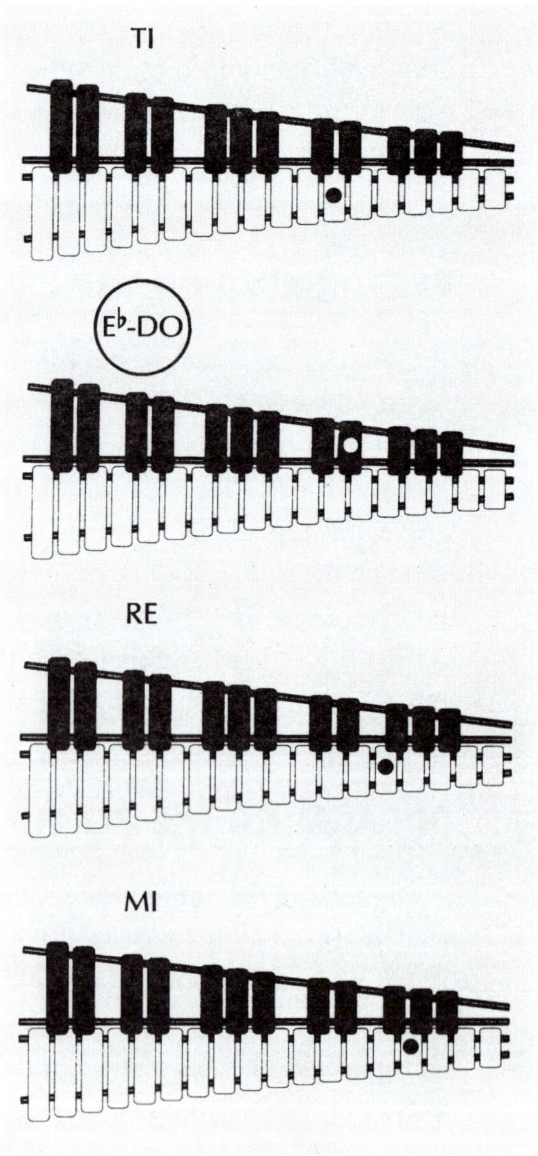

KEYBOARD ORGANIZATION

SI

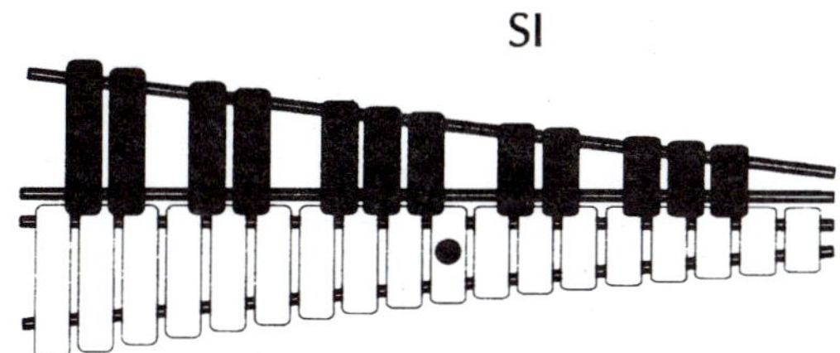

C-LA

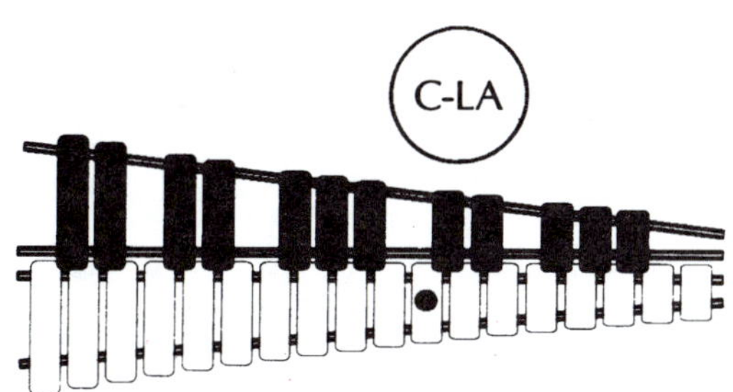

TI

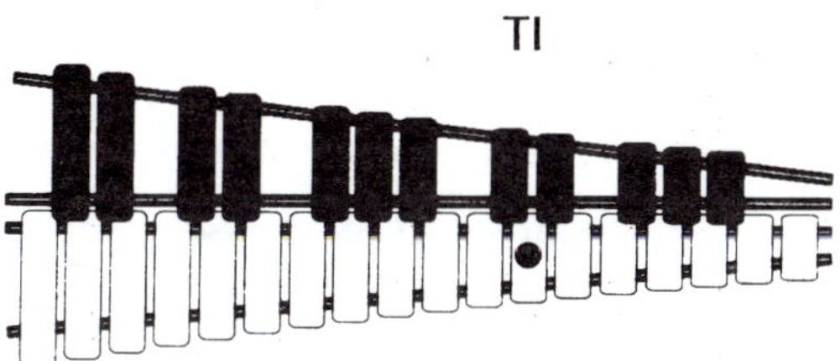

DO

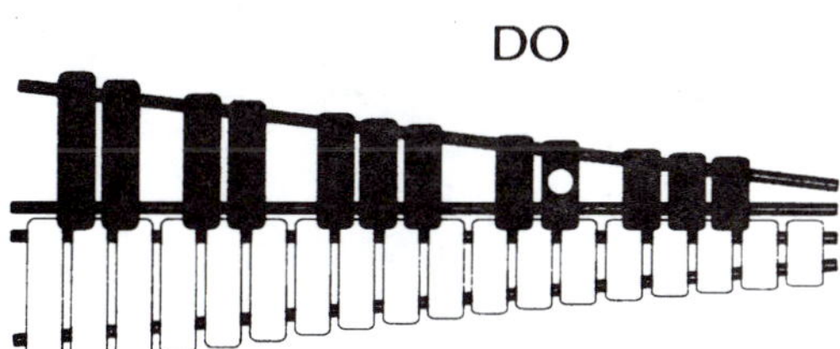

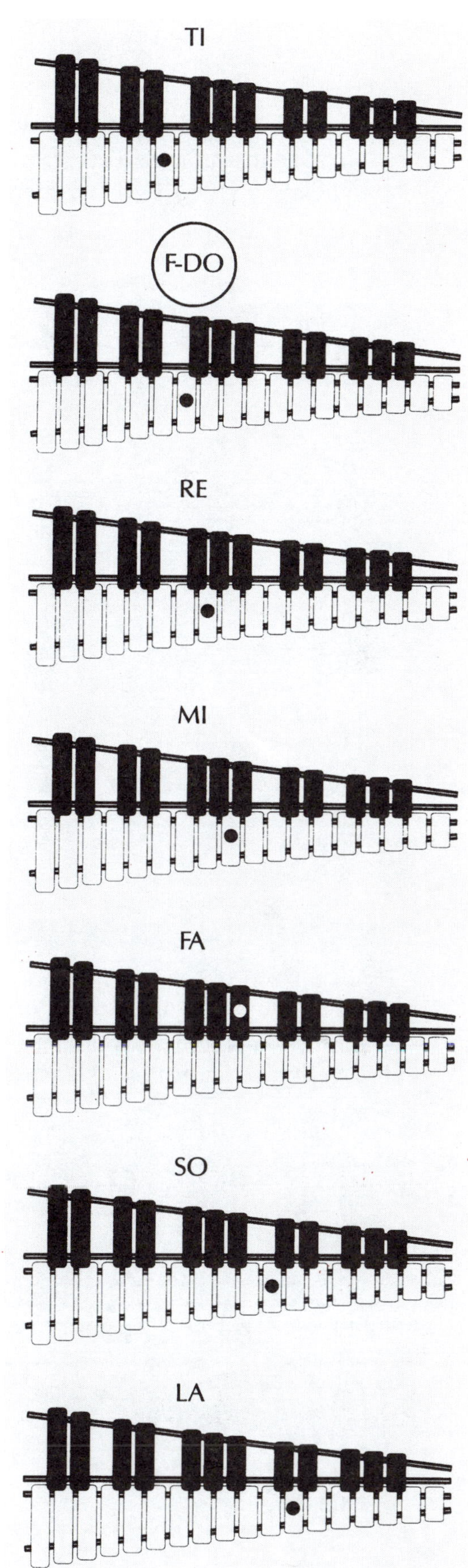

TONAL READING
TONIC AND DOMINANT FUNCTIONS IN B♭ MAJOR

1. Read the following patterns by singing them WITH TONAL SYLLABLES and by performing them on your instrument. The arrow points to DO. B♭ indicates a TONIC pattern in major tonality; F7 indicates a DOMINANT pattern in major tonality.

2. Read the following series of patterns by singing them WITH TONAL SYLLABLES and by performing them on your instrument. The arrow points to DO. B♭ indicates a TONIC pattern in major tonality; F7 indicates a DOMINANT pattern in major tonality.

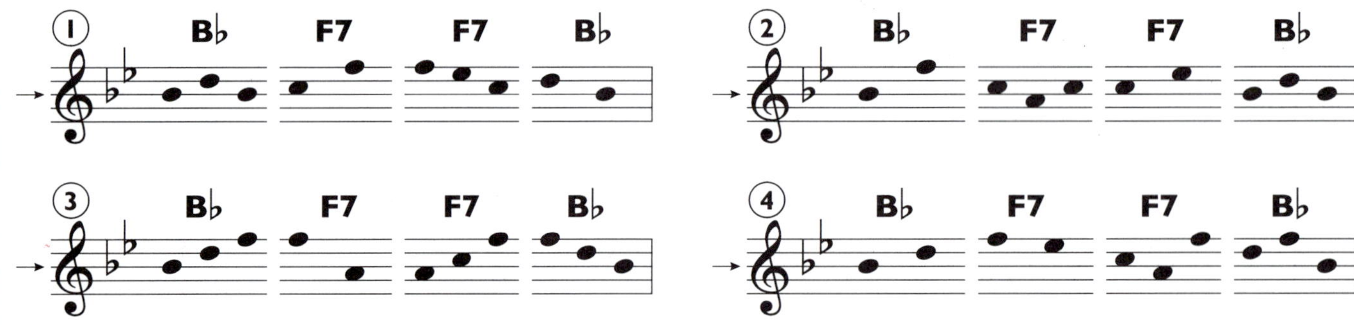

Be expressive when performing with your voice and with your instrument!

RHYTHM READING
MACROBEATS AND MICROBEATS IN DUPLE METER

1. Read the following patterns by chanting them WITH RHYTHM SYLLABLES and by performing them on your instrument.

   The number (2) tells how many macrobeats there are in a measure.
   The symbol (♩) indicates the kind of note that is a macrobeat.

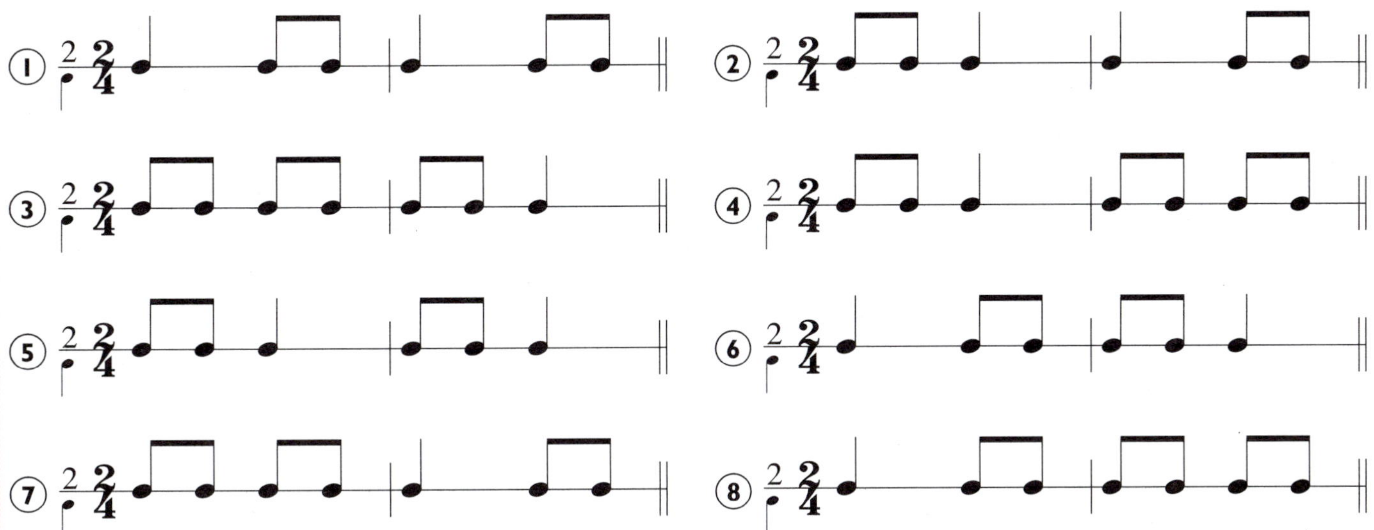

2. Read the following series of patterns by chanting them WITH RHYTHM SYLLABLES and by performing them on your instrument.

   The number (2) tells how many macrobeats there are in a measure.
   The symbol (♩) indicates the kind of note that is a macrobeat.

Be expressive when performing with your voice and with your instrument!

MAJOR DUPLE

A snare drum/bass drum part for Major Duple appears on page 24-A.

RHYTHM READING
MACROBEATS AND MICROBEATS IN TRIPLE METER

1. Read the following patterns by chanting them WITH RHYTHM SYLLABLES and by performing them on your instrument.

   The number (2) tells how many macrobeats there are in a measure.
   The symbol (♩·) indicates the kind of note that is a macrobeat.

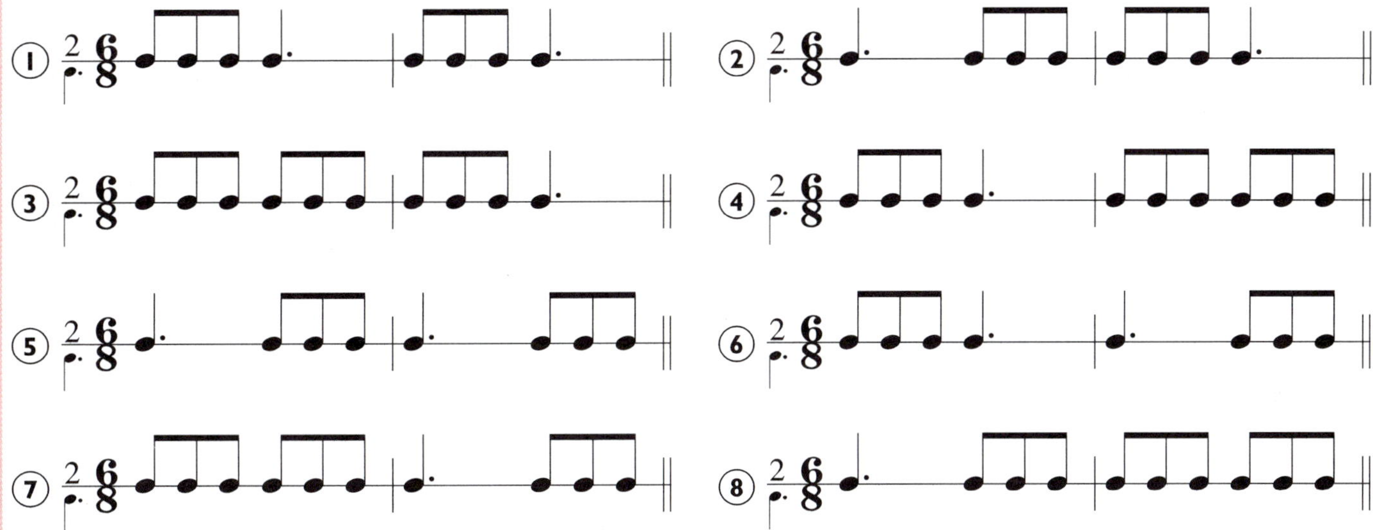

2. Read the following series of patterns by chanting them WITH RHYTHM SYLLABLES and by performing them on your instrument.

   The number (2) tells how many macrobeats there are in a measure.
   The symbol (♩·) indicates the kind of note that is a macrobeat.

Be expressive when performing with your voice and with your instrument!

MAJOR TRIPLE

A snare drum/bass drum part for Major Triple
appears on page 24-A.

ENRHYTHMIC READING
MACROBEATS AND MICROBEATS IN DUPLE METER

1. Read the following patterns by chanting them WITH RHYTHM SYLLABLES and by performing them on your instrument. The patterns on the left (4/4) are enrhythmic (they sound the same, but look different) with the patterns on the right (₵).

The numbers (4, 2) indicate how many macrobeats are in a measure.
The symbols (♩ , ♩) indicate what kind of a note is a macrobeat.

Be expressive when performing with your voice and with your instrument!

MAJOR DUPLE

A snare drum/bass drum part for Major Duple appears on page 24-A.

ENRHYTHMIC READING
MACROBEATS AND MICROBEATS IN TRIPLE METER

1. Read the following patterns by chanting them WITH RHYTHM SYLLABLES and by performing them on your instrument. The patterns on the left (3/8) are enrhythmic (they sound the same, but look different) with the patterns on the right (3/4).

   The numbers (1, 1) indicate how many macrobeats are in a measure.
   The symbols (♪. , ♩.) indicate what kind of a note is a macrobeat.

Be expressive when performing with your voice and with your instrument!

MAJOR TRIPLE

A snare drum/bass drum part for Major Triple appears on page 24-A.

TONAL READING
TONIC AND DOMINANT FUNCTIONS IN E♭ MAJOR

1. Read the following patterns by singing them WITH TONAL SYLLABLES and by performing them on your instrument. The arrow points to DO. E♭ indicates a TONIC pattern in major tonality; B♭7 indicates a DOMINANT pattern in major tonality.

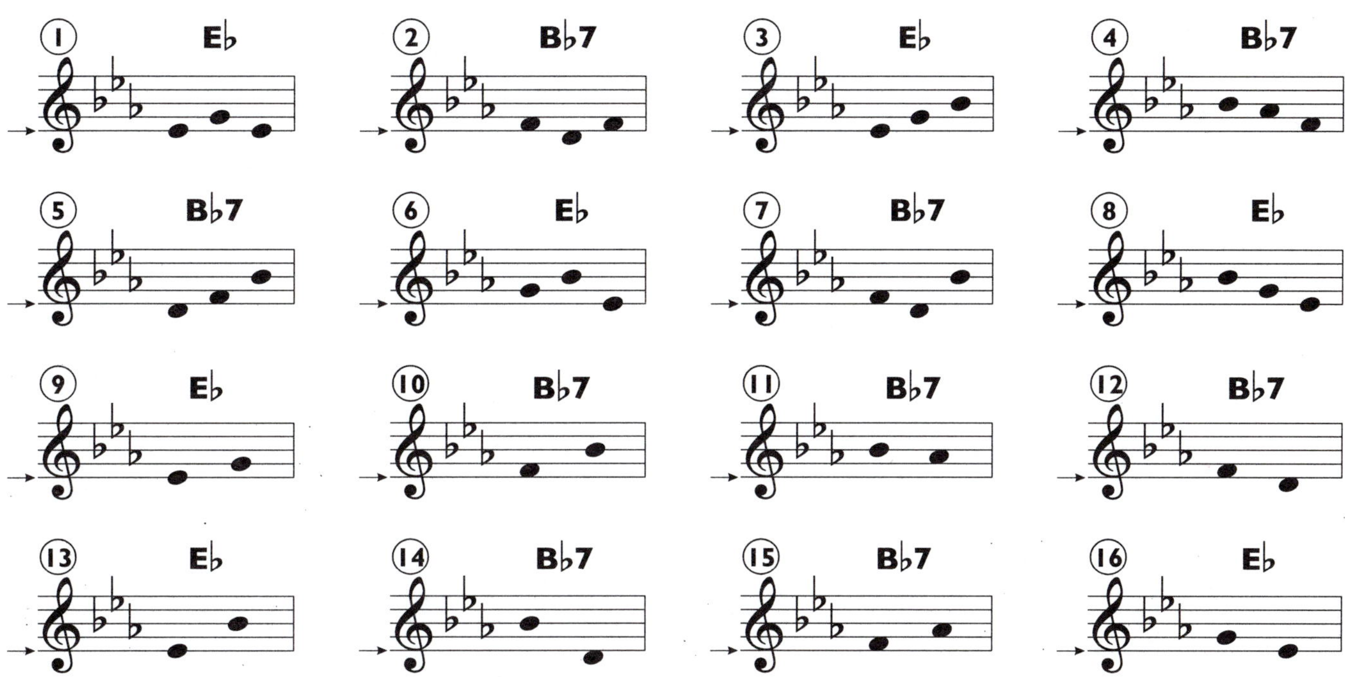

2. Read the following series of patterns by singing them WITH TONAL SYLLABLES and by performing them on your instrument. The arrow points to DO. E♭ indicates a TONIC pattern in major tonality; B♭7 indicates a DOMINANT pattern in major tonality.

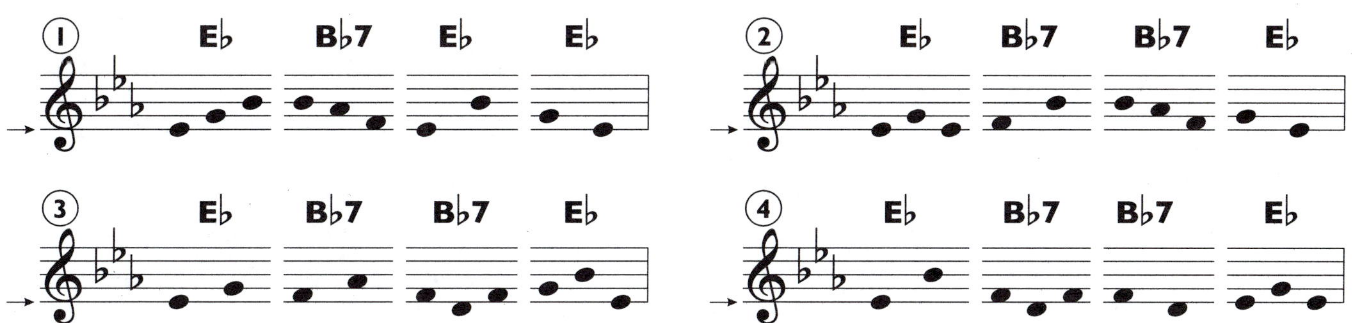

Be expressive when performing with your voice and with your instrument!

TONAL READING
TONIC, DOMINANT, AND SUBDOMINANT FUNCTIONS IN E♭ MAJOR

1. Read the following patterns by singing them WITH TONAL SYLLABLES and by performing them on your instrument. The arrow points to DO. E♭ indicates a TONIC pattern in major tonality; B♭7 indicates a DOMINANT pattern in major tonality; and A♭ indicates a SUBDOMINANT pattern in major tonality.

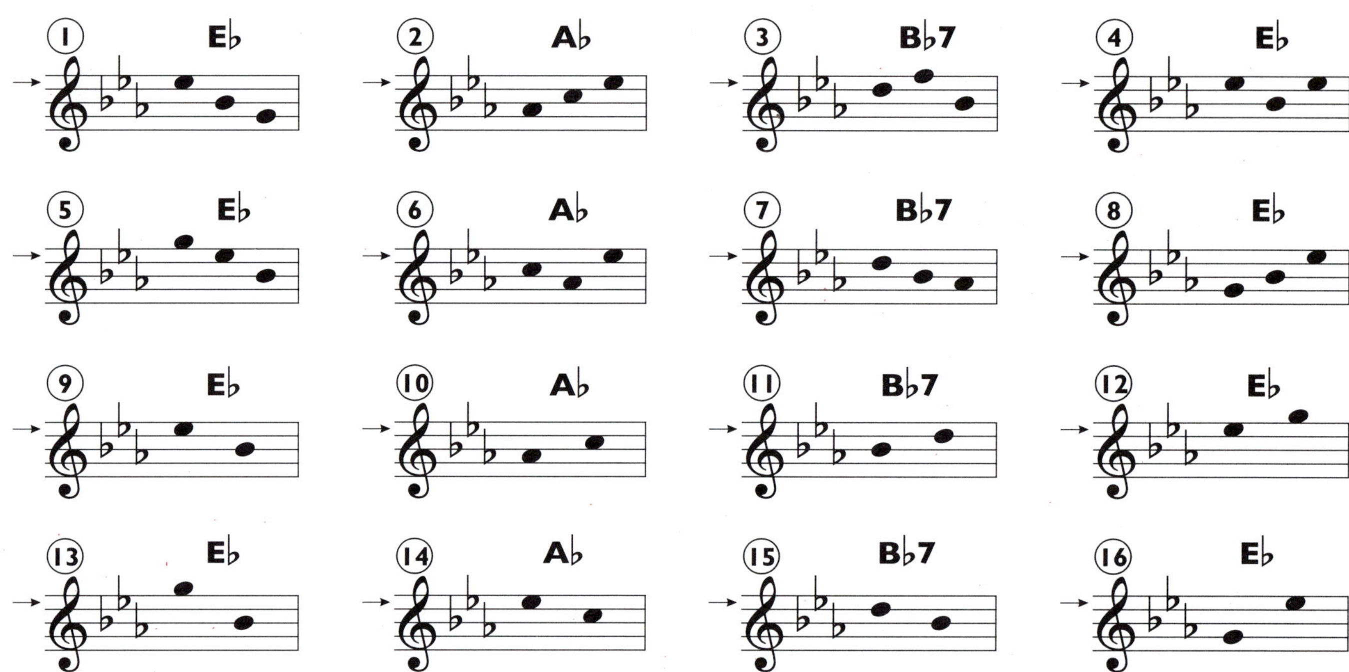

2. Read the following series of patterns by singing them WITH TONAL SYLLABLES and by performing them on your instrument. The arrow points to DO. E♭ indicates a TONIC pattern in major tonality; B♭7 indicates a DOMINANT pattern in major tonality; and A♭ indicates a SUBDOMINANT pattern in major tonality.

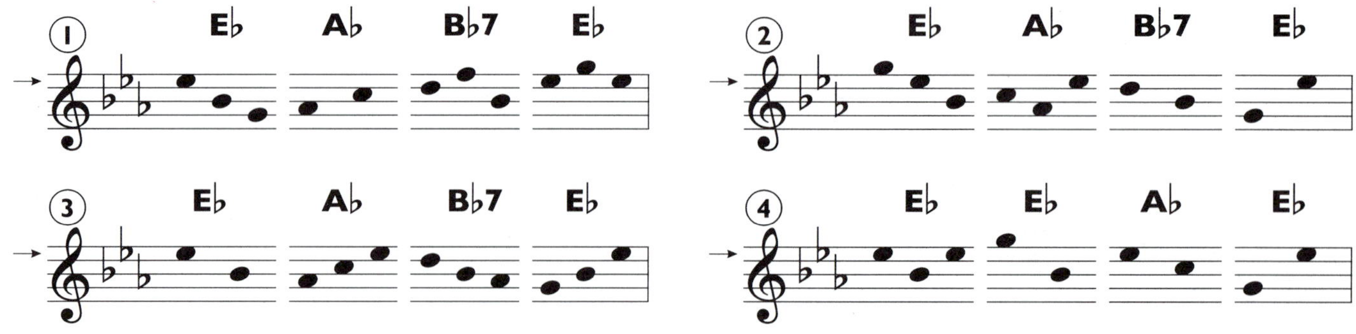

Be expressive when performing with your voice and with your instrument!

MAJOR DUPLE

A snare drum/bass drum part for Major Duple appears on page 24-A.

PIERROT

A snare drum/bass drum part for Pierrot appears on page 24-B.

TONAL READING
TONIC AND DOMINANT FUNCTIONS IN C MINOR

1. Read the following patterns by singing them WITH TONAL SYLLABLES and by performing them on your instrument. The arrow points to DO. Cm indicates a TONIC pattern in minor tonality; G7 indicates a DOMINANT pattern in minor tonality.

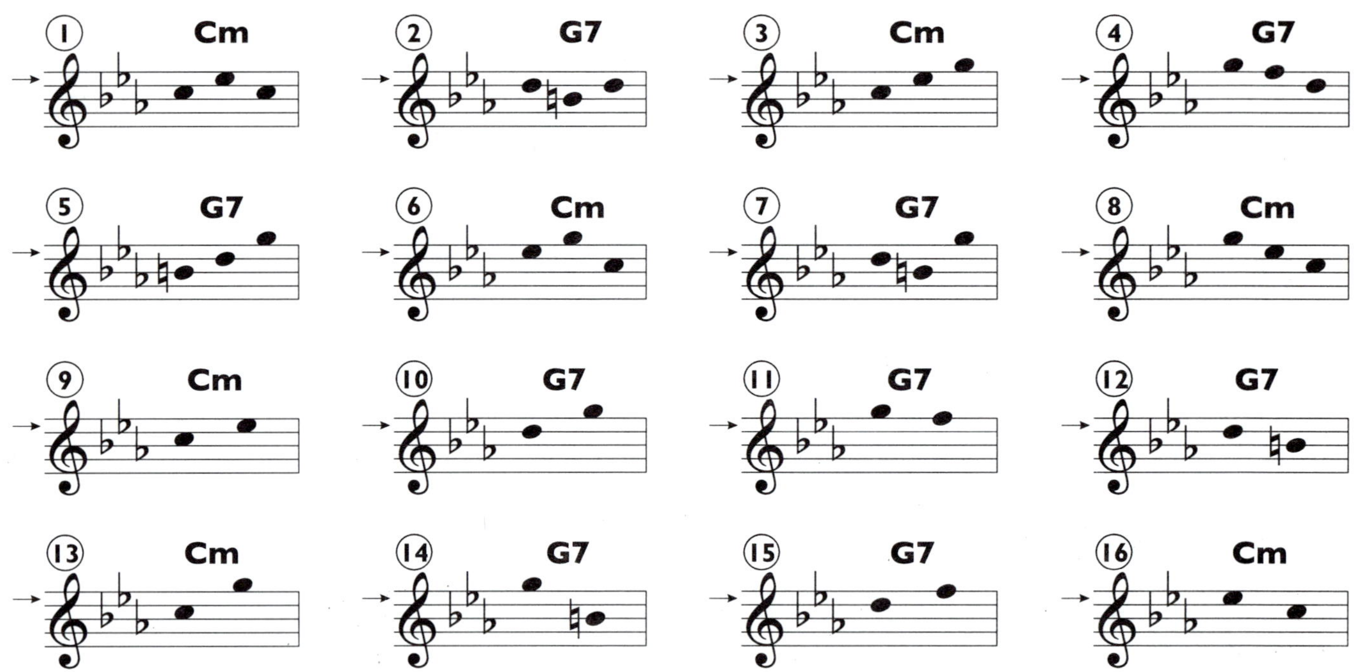

2. Read the following series of patterns by singing them WITH TONAL SYLLABLES and by performing them on your instrument. The arrow points to DO. Cm indicates a TONIC pattern in minor tonality; G7 indicates a DOMINANT pattern in minor tonality.

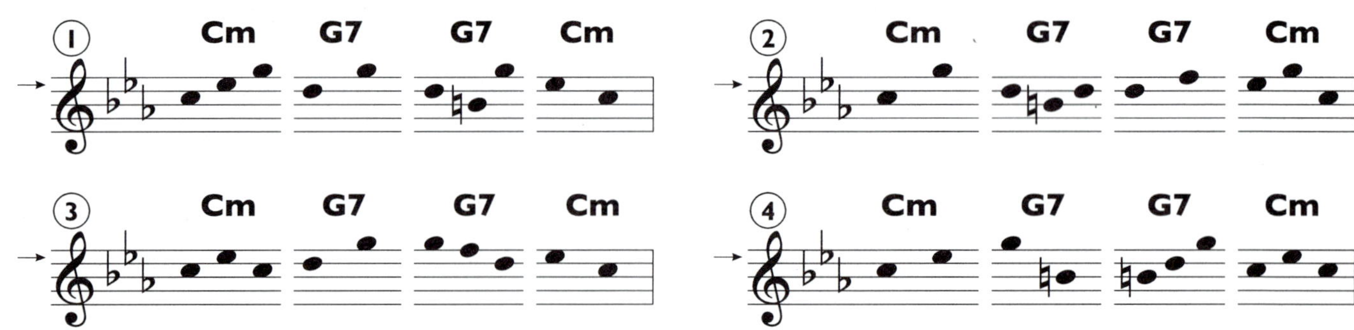

Be expressive when performing with your voice and with your instrument!

MINOR DUPLE

A snare drum/bass drum part for Minor Duple appears on page 24-B.

MINOR TRIPLE

A snare drum/bass drum part for Minor Triple appears on page 24-B.

(♩. = 72)

Melody

1

2

3

4

5

6

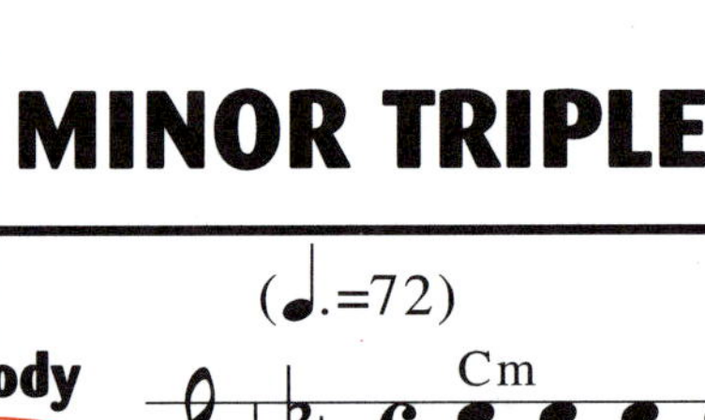

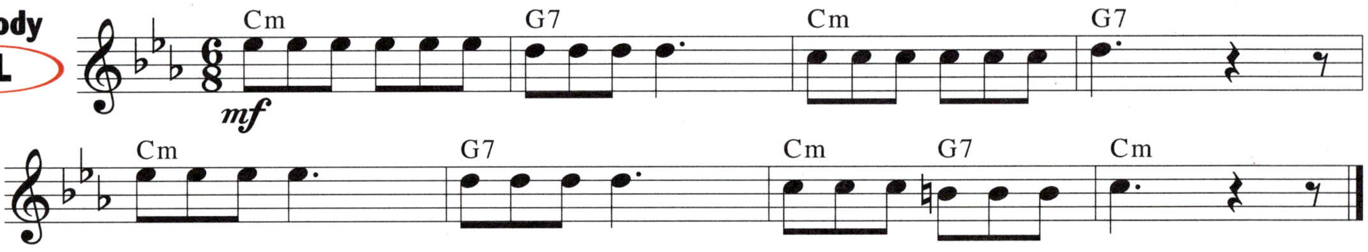

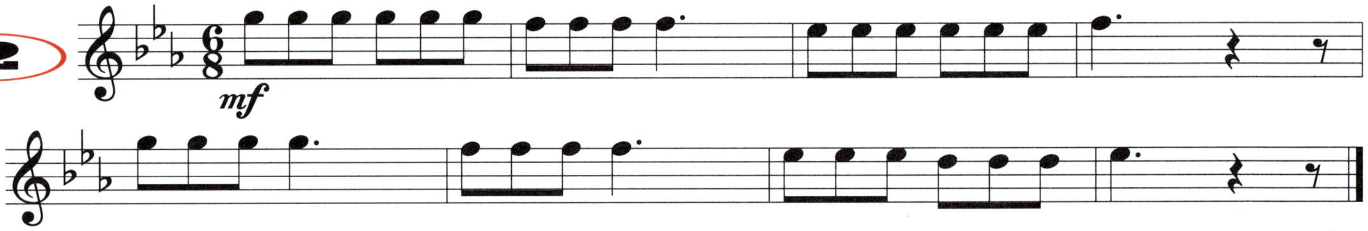

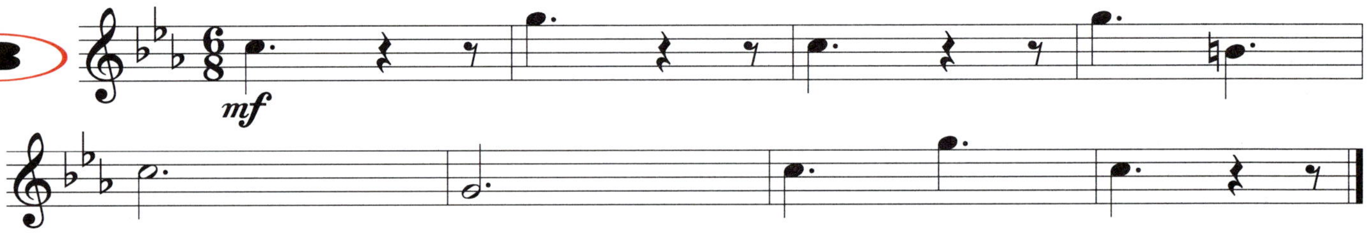

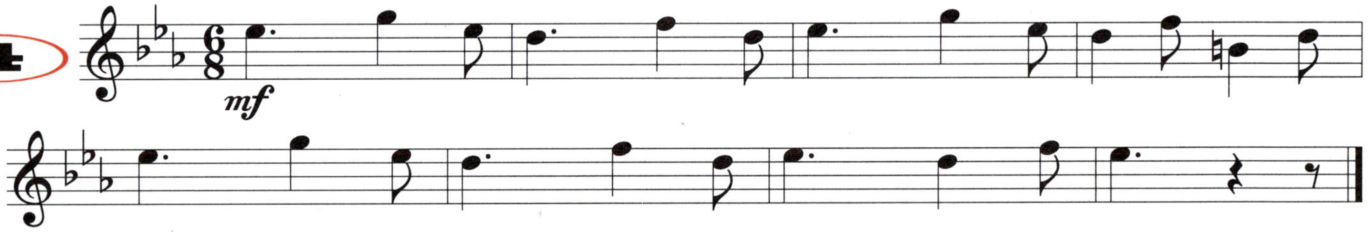

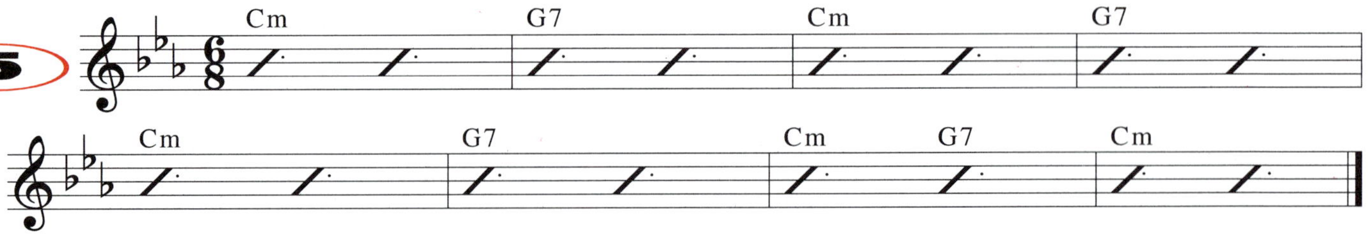

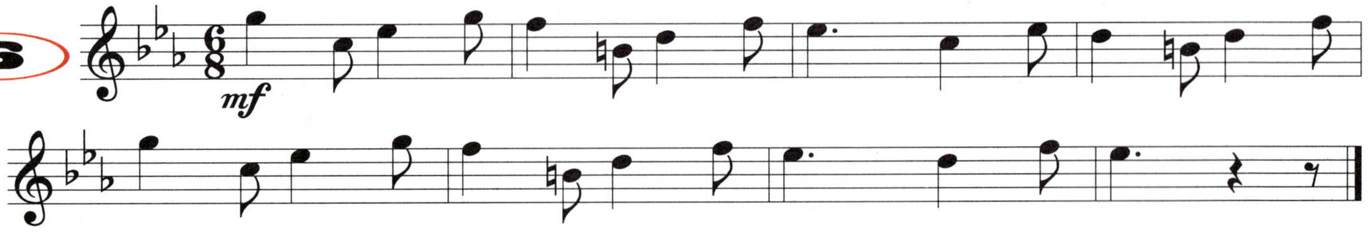

SNARE DRUM/BASS DRUM PARTS

MAJOR DUPLE (p. 12) (♩=100)

MAJOR TRIPLE (p. 14) (♩.=72)

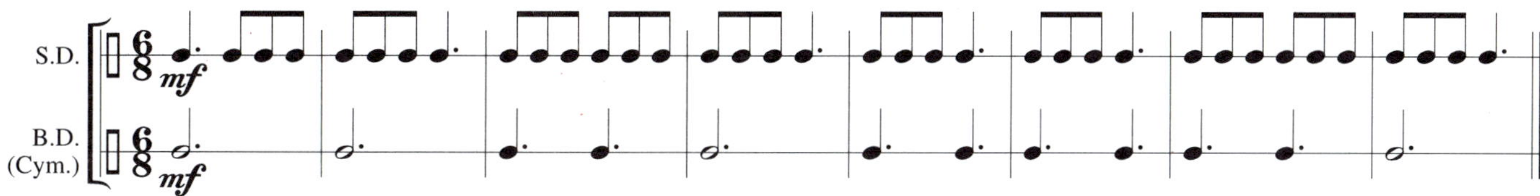

MAJOR DUPLE (p. 16) (𝅗𝅥=100)

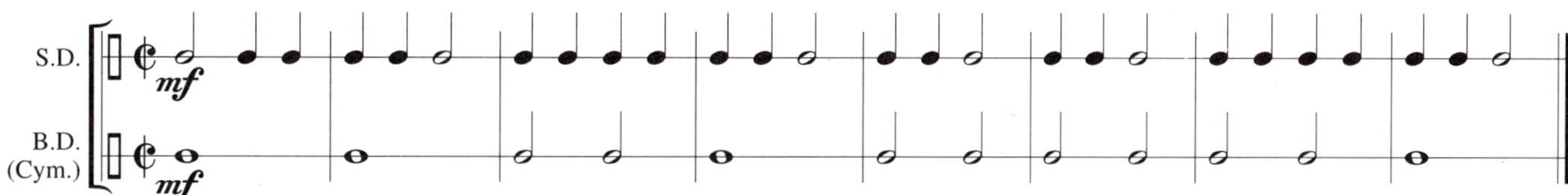

MAJOR TRIPLE (p. 18) (𝅗𝅥.=72)

MAJOR DUPLE (p. 21) (♩=100)

PIERROT (p. 21) (♩=76)

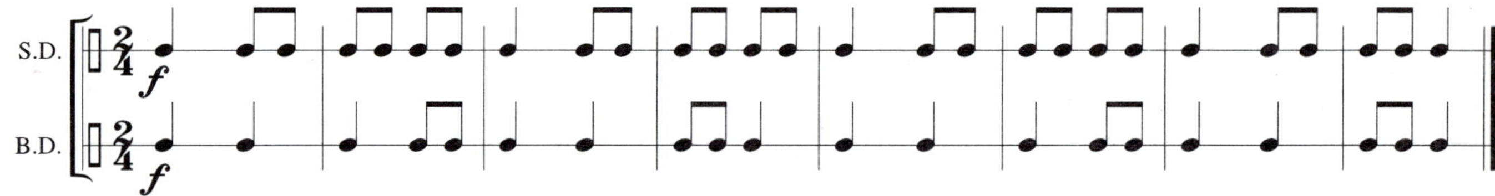

MINOR DUPLE (p. 23) (♩=100)

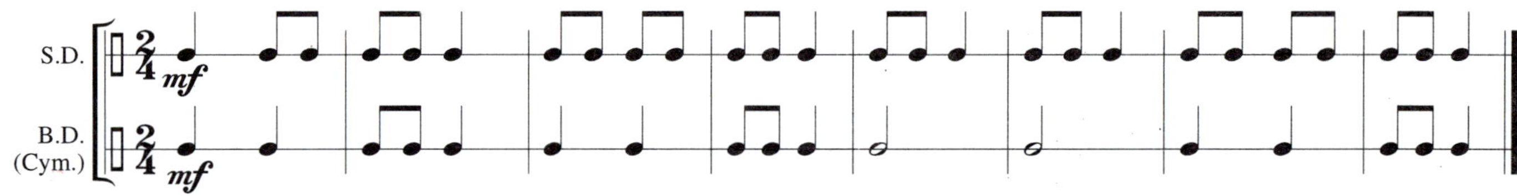

MINOR TRIPLE (p. 24) (♩.=72)

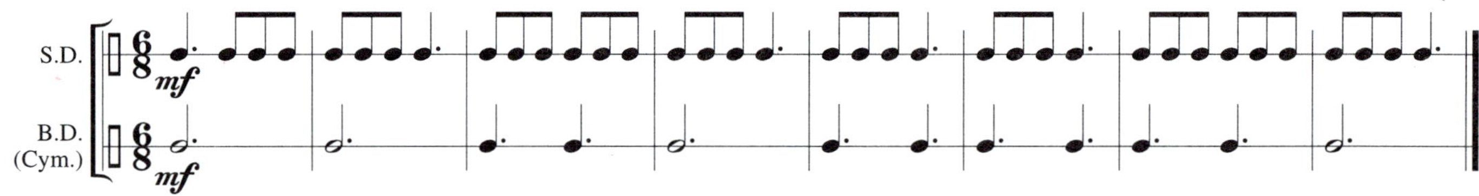

GO TELL AUNT RHODY (p. 28) (♩=100)

HOT CROSS BUNS (p. 28) (♩=66)

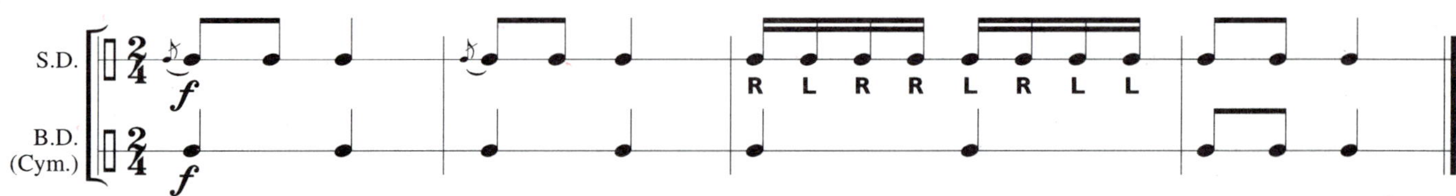

TWINKLE, TWINKLE, LITTLE STAR (p. 29) (♩=100)

TRIPLE TWINKLE (p. 30) (♩.=63)

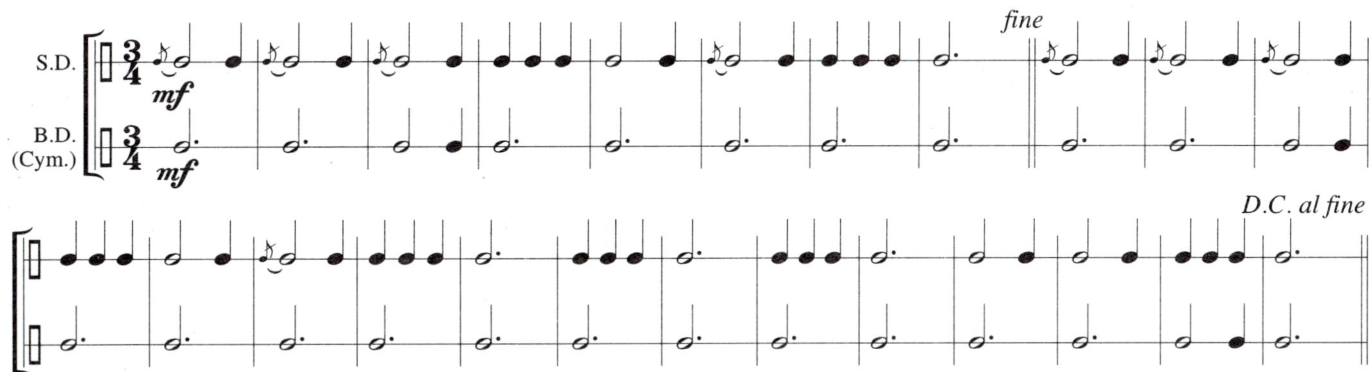

DOWN BY THE STATION (p. 34) (♩=120)

MINOR AUNT RHODY (p. 35) (♩=88)

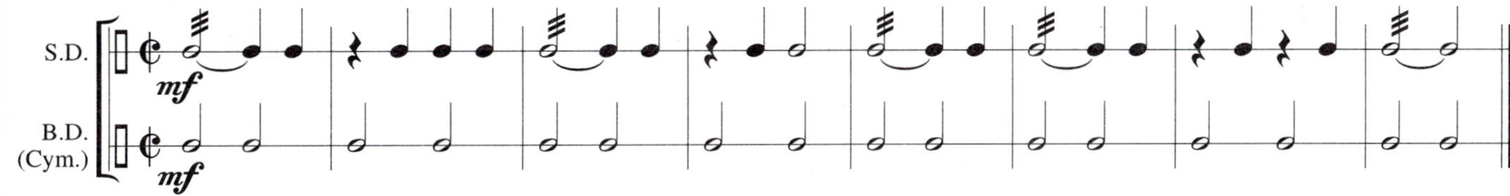

TRIPLE PIERROT (p. 35) (♩=100)

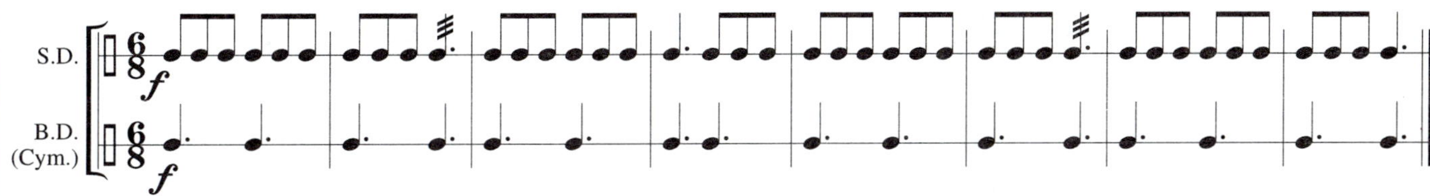

LIGHTLY ROW (p. 38) (♩=100)

BAA, BAA, BLACK SHEEP (p. 39) (♩=72)

PATSY, ORY, ORY, AYE (p. 42) (♩.=116)

OATS, PEAS, BEANS (p. 43) (♩.=108)

RHYTHM READING
MACROBEATS, MICROBEATS, AND DIVISIONS IN DUPLE METER

1. Read the following patterns by chanting them WITH RHYTHM SYLLABLES and by performing them on your instrument.

   The number (2) tells how many macrobeats there are in a measure.
   The symbol (♩) indicates the kind of note that is a macrobeat.

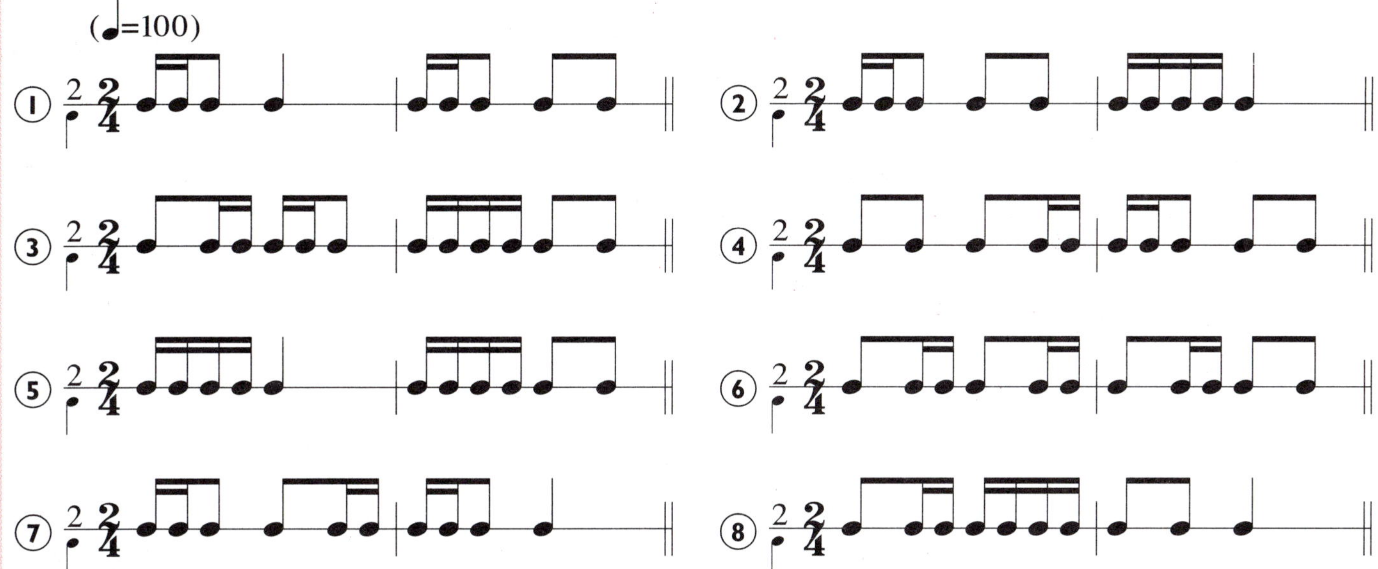

2. Read the following series of patterns by chanting them WITH RHYTHM SYLLABLES and by performing them on your instrument.

   The number (2) tells how many macrobeats there are in a measure.
   The symbol (♩) indicates the kind of note that is a macrobeat.

Be expressive when performing with your voice and with your instrument!

TONAL READING
TONIC AND DOMINANT FUNCTIONS IN F MAJOR

1. Read the following patterns by singing them WITH TONAL SYLLABLES and by performing them on your instrument. The arrow points to DO. F indicates a TONIC pattern in major tonality; C7 indicates a DOMINANT pattern in major tonality.

2. Read the following series of patterns by singing them WITH TONAL SYLLABLES and by performing them on your instrument. The arrow points to DO. F indicates a TONIC pattern in major tonality; C7 indicates a DOMINANT pattern in major tonality.

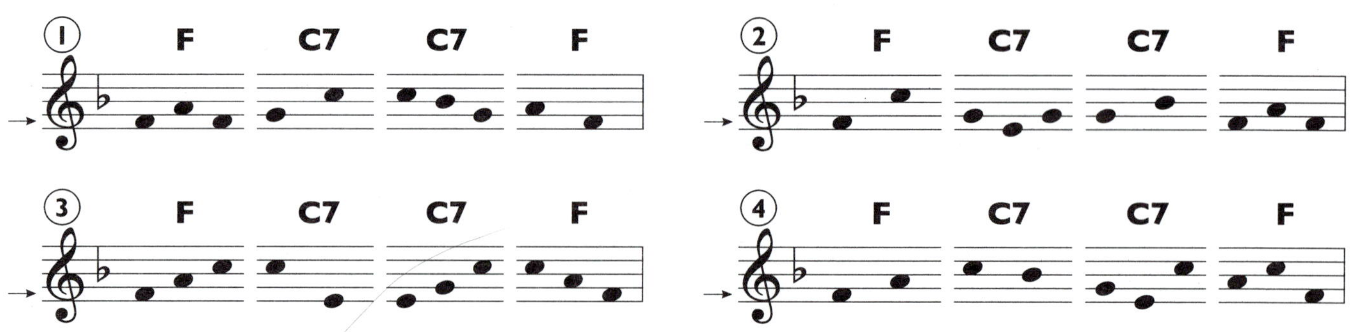

Be expressive when performing with your voice and with your instrument!

TONAL READING
TONIC, DOMINANT, AND SUBDOMINANT FUNCTIONS IN F MAJOR

1. Read the following patterns by singing them WITH TONAL SYLLABLES and by performing them on your instrument. The arrow points to DO. F indicates a TONIC pattern in major tonality; C7 indicates a DOMINANT pattern in major tonality; and B♭ indicates a SUBDOMINANT pattern in major tonality.

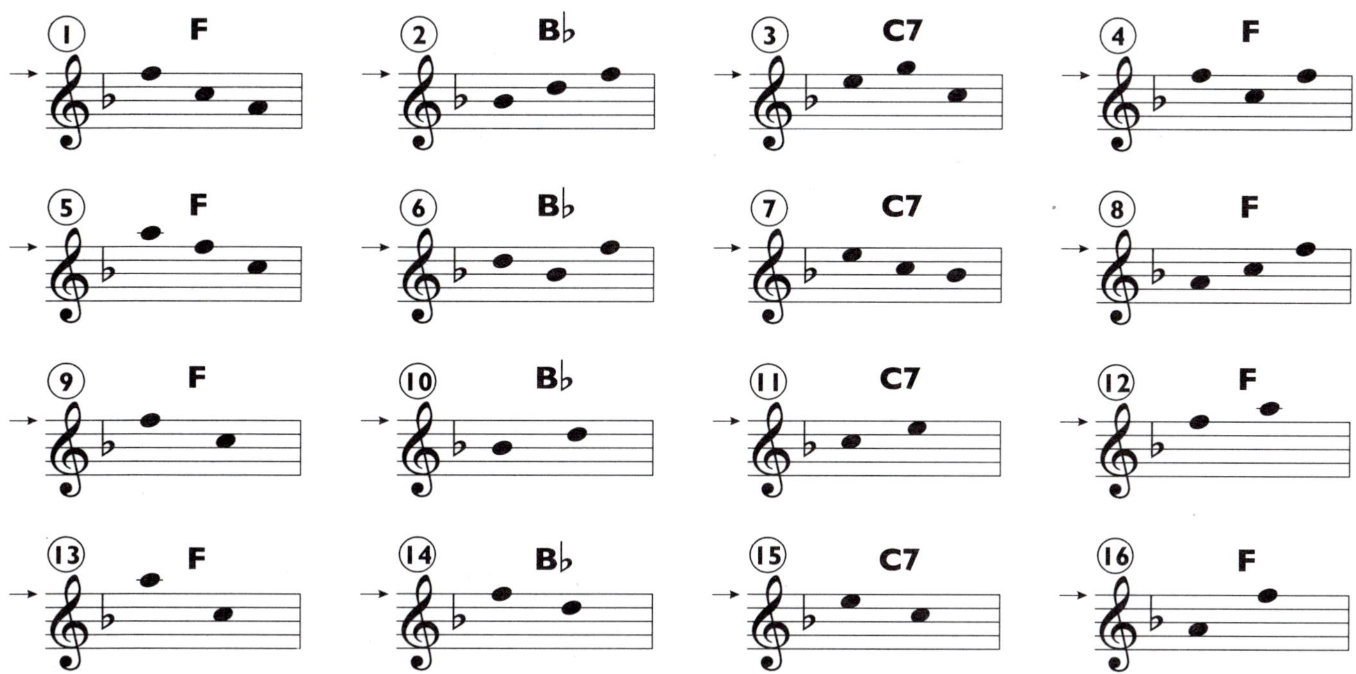

2. Read the following series of patterns by singing them WITH TONAL SYLLABLES and by performing them on your instrument. The arrow points to DO. F indicates a TONIC pattern in major tonality; C7 indicates a DOMINANT pattern in major tonality; and B♭ indicates a SUBDOMINANT pattern in major tonality.

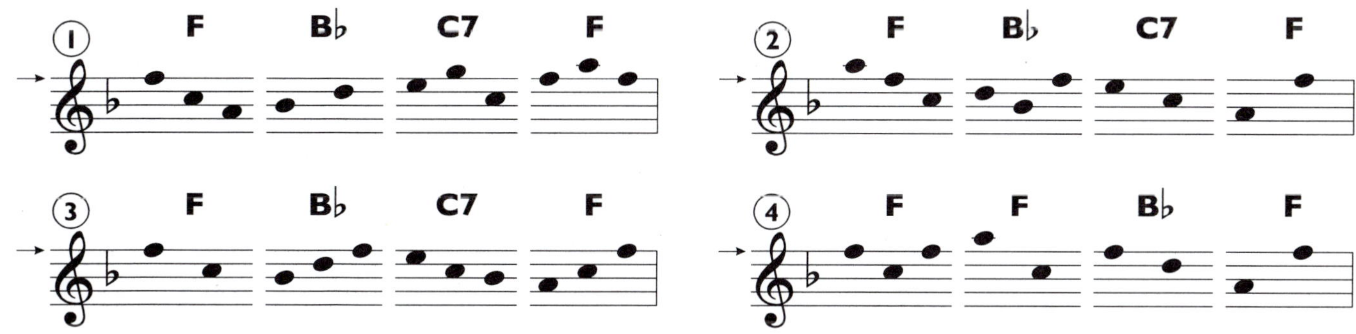

Be expressive when performing with your voice and with your instrument!

GO TELL AUNT RHODY

A snare drum/bass drum part for Go Tell Aunt Rhody appears on page 24-B.

HOT CROSS BUNS

A snare drum/bass drum part for Hot Cross Buns appears on page 24-B.

TWINKLE, TWINKLE, LITTLE STAR

A snare drum/bass drum part for Twinkle, Twinkle, Little Star appears on page 24-C.

TRIPLE TWINKLE

A snare drum/bass drum part for Triple Twinkle appears on page 24-C.

ENRHYTHMIC READING
MACROBEATS, MICROBEATS, AND DIVISIONS IN DUPLE METER

1. Read the following patterns by chanting them WITH RHYTHM SYLLABLES and by performing them on your instrument. The patterns on the left (4/4) are enrhythmic (they sound the same, but look different) with the patterns on the right (₵).

The numbers (4, 2) indicate how many macrobeats are in a measure.
The symbols (♩ , ♪) indicate what kind of a note is a macrobeat.

RHYTHM READING
MACROBEATS, MICROBEATS, AND DIVISIONS IN TRIPLE METER

CD track 77

1. Read the following patterns by chanting them WITH RHYTHM SYLLABLES and by performing them on your instrument.

   The number (2) tells how many macrobeats there are in a measure.
   The symbol (♩·) indicates the kind of note that is a macrobeat.

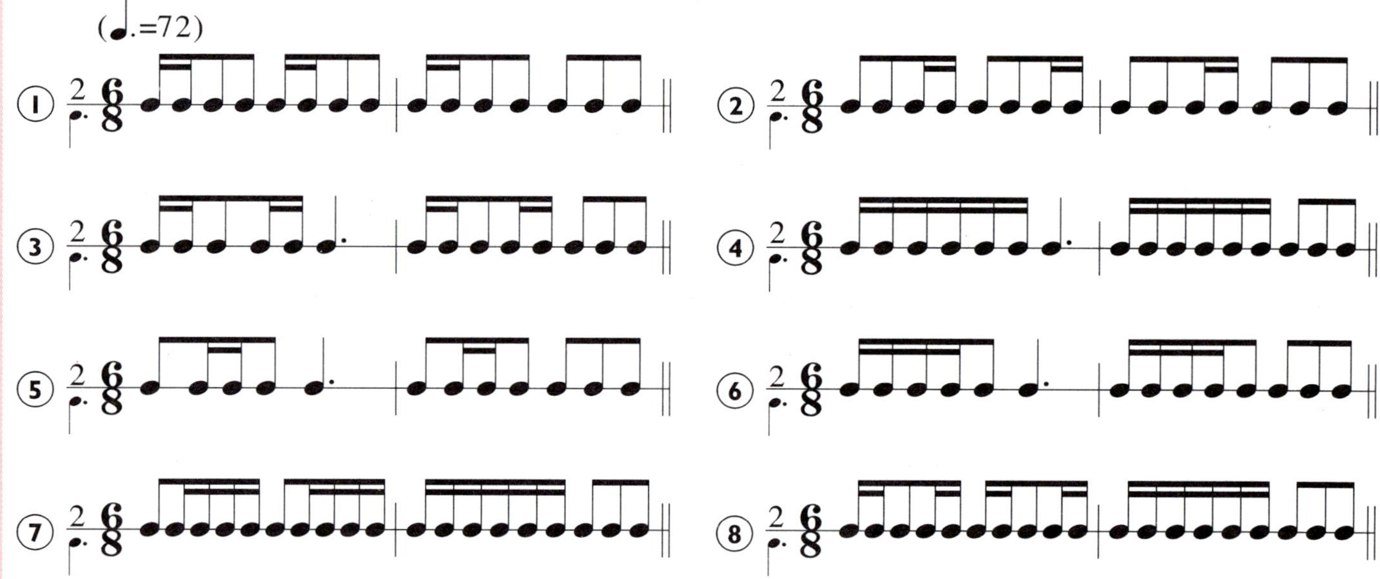

2. Read the following series of patterns by chanting them WITH RHYTHM SYLLABLES and by performing them on your instrument.

   The number (2) tells how many macrobeats there are in a measure.
   The symbol (♩·) indicates the kind of note that is a macrobeat.

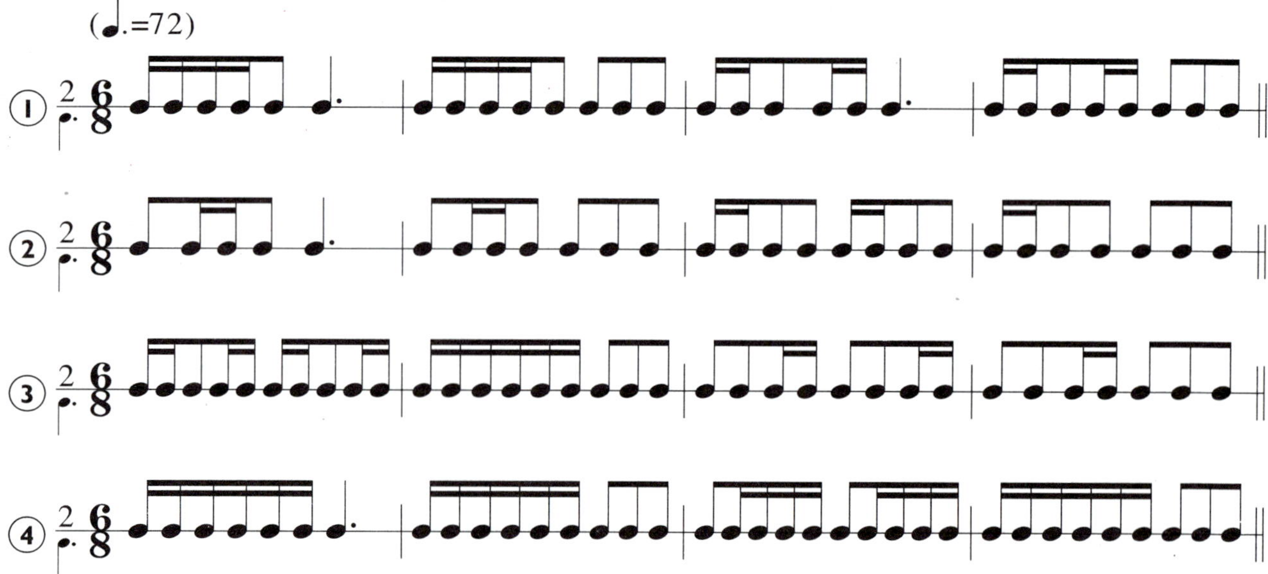

Be expressive when performing with your voice and with your instrument!

ENRHYTHMIC READING
MACROBEATS, MICROBEATS, AND DIVISIONS IN TRIPLE METER

1. Read the following patterns by chanting them WITH RHYTHM SYLLABLES and by performing them on your instrument. The patterns on the left (3/8) are enrhythmic (they sound the same, but look different) with the patterns on the right (3/4).

The numbers (1, 1) indicate how many macrobeats are in a measure.
The symbols (♪. , ♩.) indicate what kind of a note is a macrobeat.

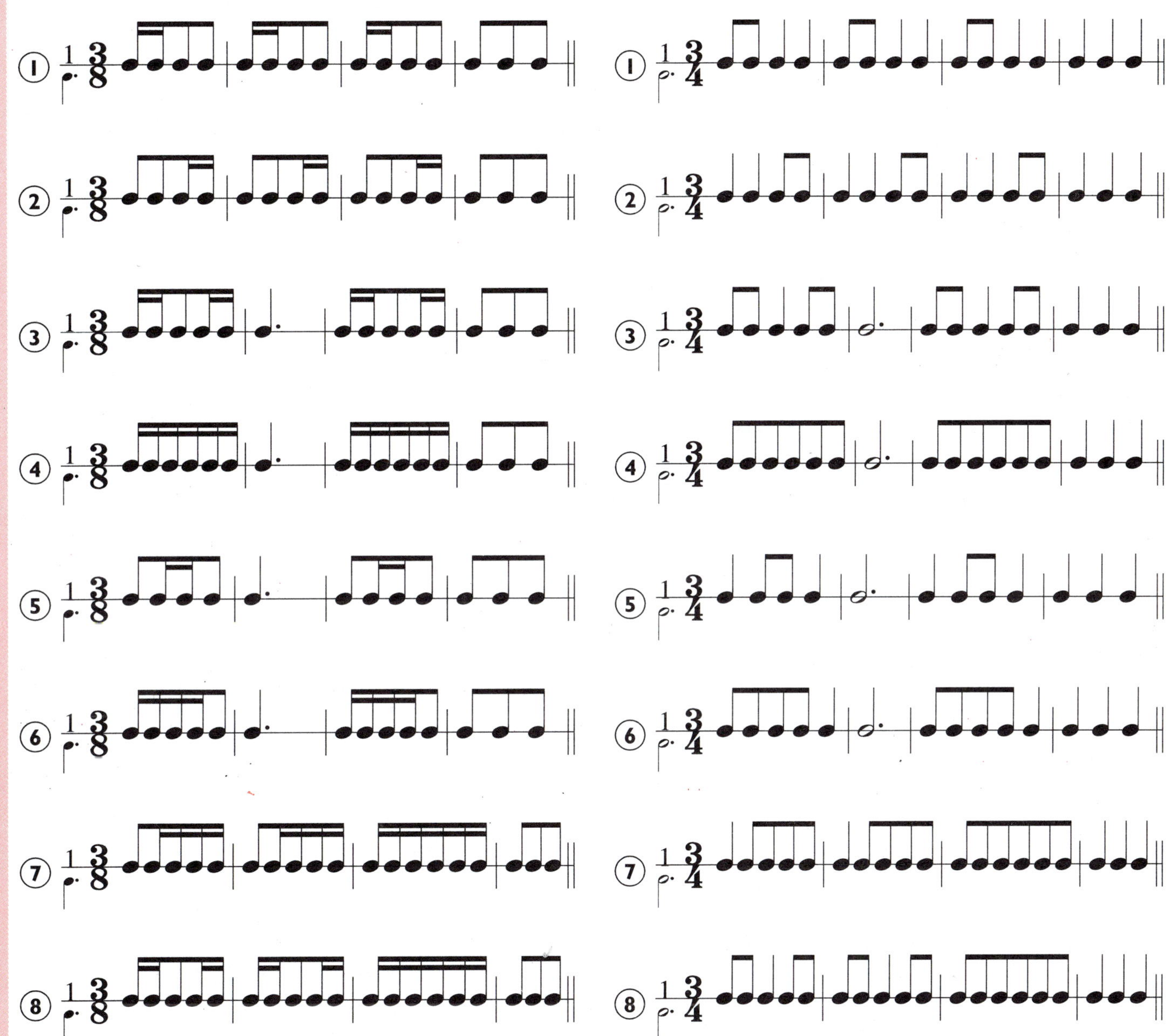

DOWN BY THE STATION

*A snare drum/bass drum part for Down
By the Station appears on page 24-C.*

MINOR AUNT RHODY

A snare drum/bass drum part for Minor Aunt Rhody appears on page 24-C.

TRIPLE PIERROT

A snare drum/bass drum part for Triple Pierrot appears on page 24-C.

RHYTHM READING
MACROBEATS, MICROBEATS, DIVISIONS, AND ELONGATIONS IN DUPLE METER

1. Read the following patterns by chanting them WITH RHYTHM SYLLABLES and by performing them on your instrument.

   The number (2) tells how many macrobeats there are in a measure.
   The symbol (♩) indicates the kind of note that is a macrobeat.

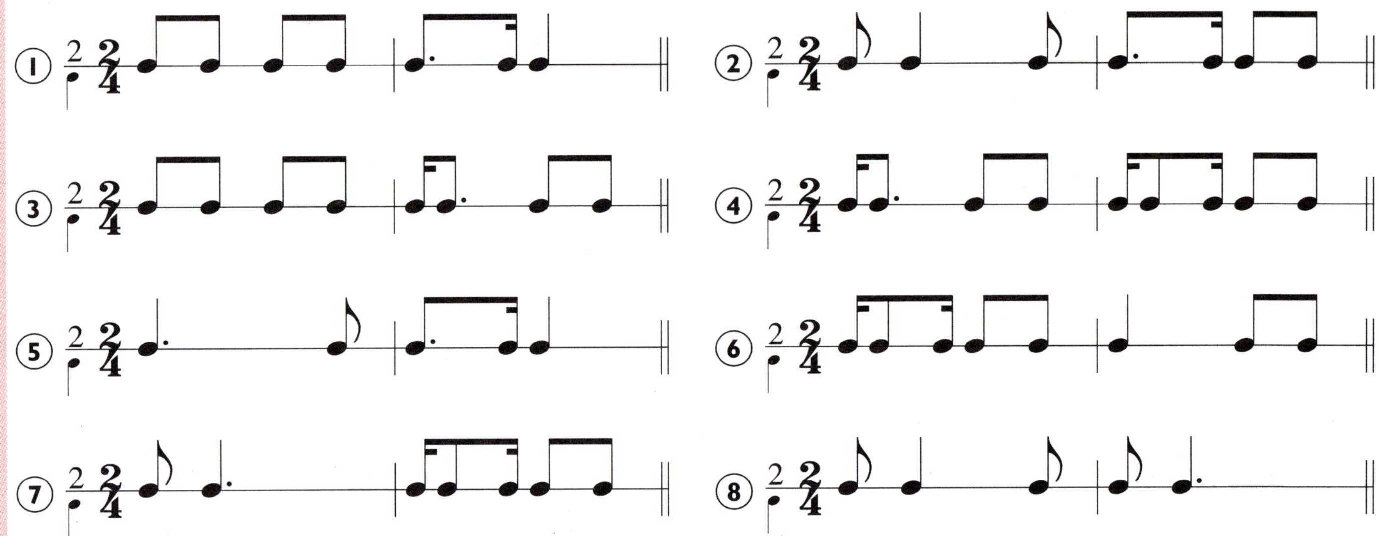

2. Read the following series of patterns by chanting them WITH RHYTHM SYLLABLES and by performing them on your instrument.

   The number (2) tells how many macrobeats there are in a measure.
   The symbol (♩) indicates the kind of note that is a macrobeat.

Be expressive when performing with your voice and with your instrument!

ENRHYTHMIC READING
MACROBEATS, MICROBEATS, DIVISIONS, AND ELONGATIONS IN DUPLE METER

1. Read the following patterns by chanting them WITH RHYTHM SYLLABLES and by performing them on your instrument. The patterns on the left (4/4) are enrhythmic (they sound the same, but look different) with the patterns on the right (¢).

The numbers (4, 2) indicate how many macrobeats are in a measure.
The symbols (♩ , ♩) indicate what kind of a note is a macrobeat.

Be expressive when performing with your voice and with your instrument!

LIGHTLY ROW

A snare drum/bass drum part for Lightly Row appears on page 24-D.

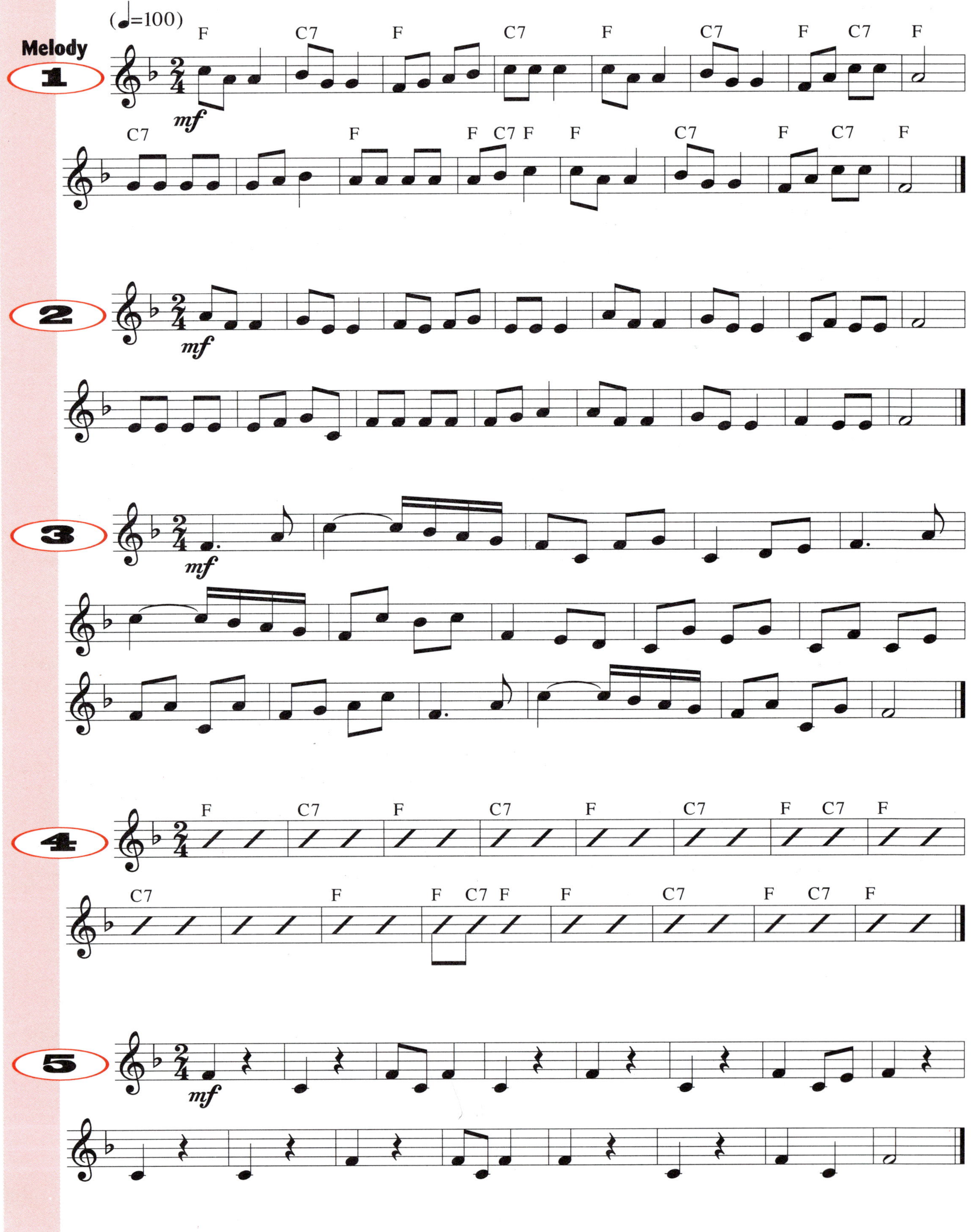

BAA, BAA, BLACK SHEEP

A snare drum/bass drum part for Baa, Baa, Black Sheep appears on page 24-D.

RHYTHM READING
MACROBEATS, MICROBEATS, DIVISIONS, AND ELONGATIONS IN TRIPLE METER

1. Read the following patterns by chanting them WITH RHYTHM SYLLABLES and by performing them on your instrument.

   The number (2) tells how many macrobeats there are in a measure.
   The symbol (♩.) indicates the kind of note that is a macrobeat.

2. Read the following series of patterns by chanting them WITH RHYTHM SYLLABLES and by performing them on your instrument.

   The number (2) tells how many macrobeats there are in a measure.
   The symbol (♩.) indicates the kind of note that is a macrobeat.

Be expressive when performing with your voice and with your instrument!

ENRHYTHMIC READING
MACROBEATS, MICROBEATS, DIVISIONS, AND ELONGATIONS IN TRIPLE METER

1. Read the following patterns by chanting them **WITH RHYTHM SYLLABLES** and by performing them on your instrument. The patterns on the left (3/8) are enrhythmic (they sound the same, but look different) with the patterns on the right (3/4).

The numbers (1, 1) indicate how many macrobeats are in a measure.
The symbols (♩. , ♩.) indicate what kind of a note is a macrobeat.

Be expressive when performing with your voice and with your instrument!

PATSY, ORY, ORY, AYE

A snare drum/bass drum part for Patsy, Ory, Ory, Aye appears on page 24-D.

OATS, PEAS, BEANS

A snare drum/bass drum part for Oats, Peas, Beans appears on page 24-D.

TONAL SIGHT READING

1. Sight read the following patterns by singing them WITH A NEUTRAL SYLLABLE and by performing them on your instrument. Some of the patterns are familiar and some are unfamiliar. The arrow points to DO.

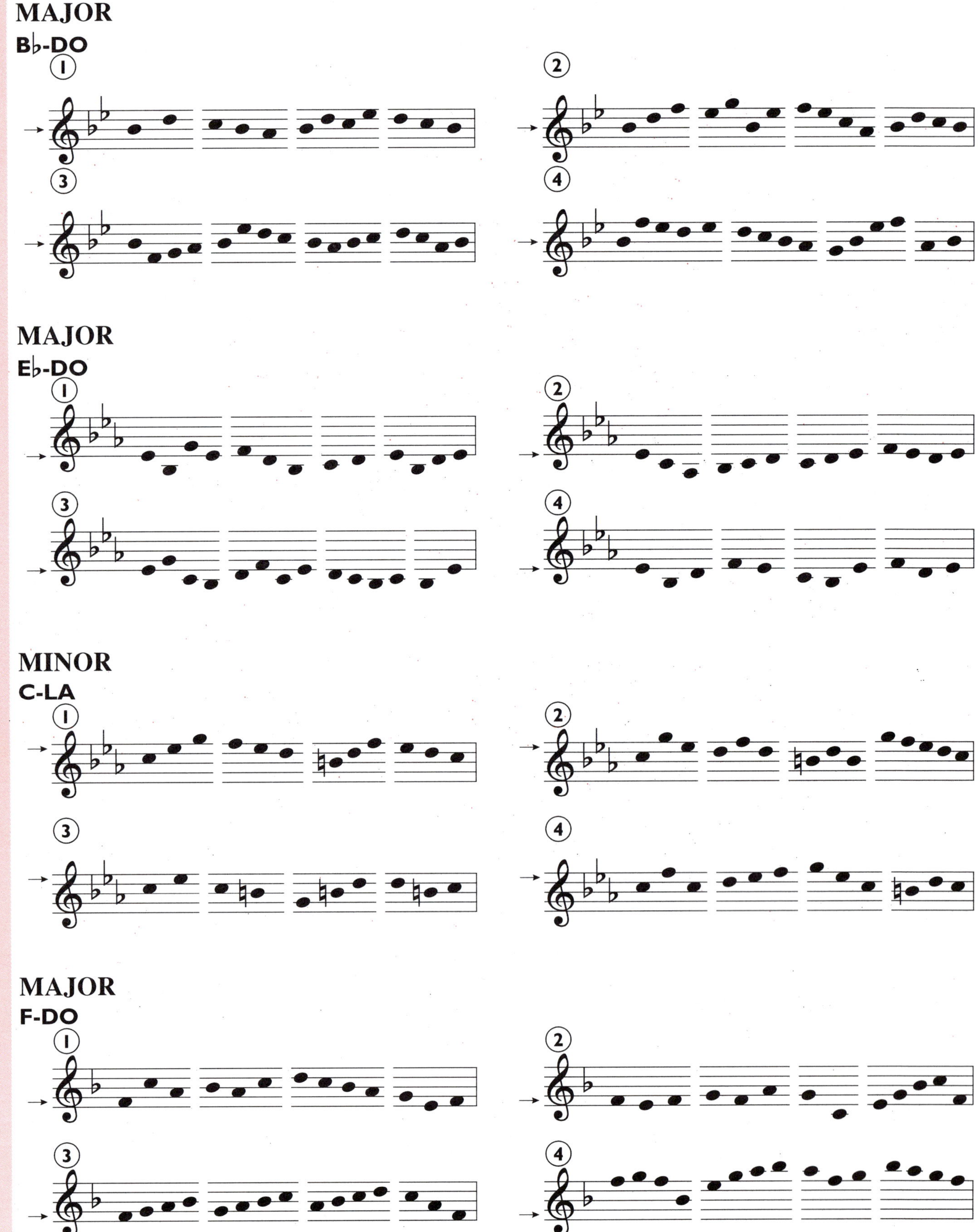

RHYTHM SIGHT READING

1. Sight read the following rhythm patterns by chanting them WITH A NEUTRAL SYLLABLE and by performing them on your instrument. Some of the patterns are familiar and some are unfamiliar.

    The number (2) tells how many macrobeats there are in a measure.
    The symbol (♩ or ♩.) indicates the kind of note that is a macrobeat.

DUPLE

TRIPLE

MELODIC SIGHT READING

1. Audiate one of the following melodies. If necessary, SING INDIVIDUAL TONAL PATTERNS WITH TONAL SYLLABLES, and CHANT INDIVIDUAL RHYTHM PATTERNS WITH RHYTHM SYLLABLES. DO NOT SING THE ENTIRE MELODY WITH TONAL SYLLABLES. YOU MAY CHANT THE ENTIRE MELODIC RHYTHM USING RHYTHM SYLLABLES.

2. Audiate that melody while performing it silently on your instrument.

3. Perform that melody on your instrument.

MUSICAL ENRICHMENT

"Musical Enrichment" begins with item #94 on the *Home-Study Compact Disc*. Listen Carefully as a professional musician performs some familiar folk songs. Before each performance the announcer will give the resting tone and starting pitch. For example:

"B♭ is DO, start on DO," indicates that
   1) B♭ is the resting tone,
   2) the song is in major tonality (because DO is the resting tone), and
   3) the song begins on DO.

"C is LA, start on MI," indicates that
   1) C is the resting tone,
   2) the song is in minor tonality (because LA is the resting tone), and
   3) the song begins on MI.

Listen many times to the songs, noting the tone quality, style of articulation, and phrasing. When you can audiate a song (when you can hear it in your head), you may begin to perform that song "by ear." Some of the songs are easy and will require little time to learn to perform. Other songs are more challenging and will require more time to learn to perform. The fingering chart beginning on the next page will help you locate the appropriate DO or LA, and the correct starting pitch. Remember it is alright to make mistakes when you first play "by ear."

Musical Enrichment also includes the activities listed below. Your music teacher will help you mark the charts to indicate when you have satisfactorily completed each of the activities.

   A. Sing the song with or without words.
   B. Perform the song in the tonality and keyality found on the *Home-Study Compact Disc*.
   C. Perform the song in a different keyality. (Start on a different note.)
   D. Perform the song with a friend who plays the same or a different instrument.
   E. Perform the song in a different meter. (Change from duple to triple or from triple to duple.)
   F. Perform the song in a different tonality. (Change from major to minor or from minor to major.)
   G. Perform an improvisation or harmony part for the song.

Item/Track No.

1. 94. "Mary Had a Little Lamb" (B♭ is DO; start on MI) — A B C D E F G

2. 94. "London Bridge" (B♭ is DO; start on SO) — A B C D E F G

3. 94. "America" (B♭ is DO; start on DO) — A B C D E F G

4. 95. "Clementine" (E♭ is DO; start on DO) — A B C D E F G

5. 95. "Hot Cross Buns" (E♭ is DO; start on MI) — A B C D E F G

6. 95. "Hush Little Baby" (E♭ is DO; start on SO) — A B C D E F G

7. 96. "Coventry Carol" (C is LA; start on LA) — A B C D E F G

8. 96. "Snake Dance" (C is LA; start on LA) — A B C D E F G

9. 96. "This Ol' Hammer" (C is LA; start on LA) — A B C D E F G

10. 97. "Yankee Doodle" (F is DO; start on DO) — A B C D E F G

11. 97. "Amazing Grace" (F is DO; start on SO) — A B C D E F G

12. 97. "Sleep Baby Sleep" (F is DO; start on MI) — A B C D E F G

KEYBOARD ORGANIZATION

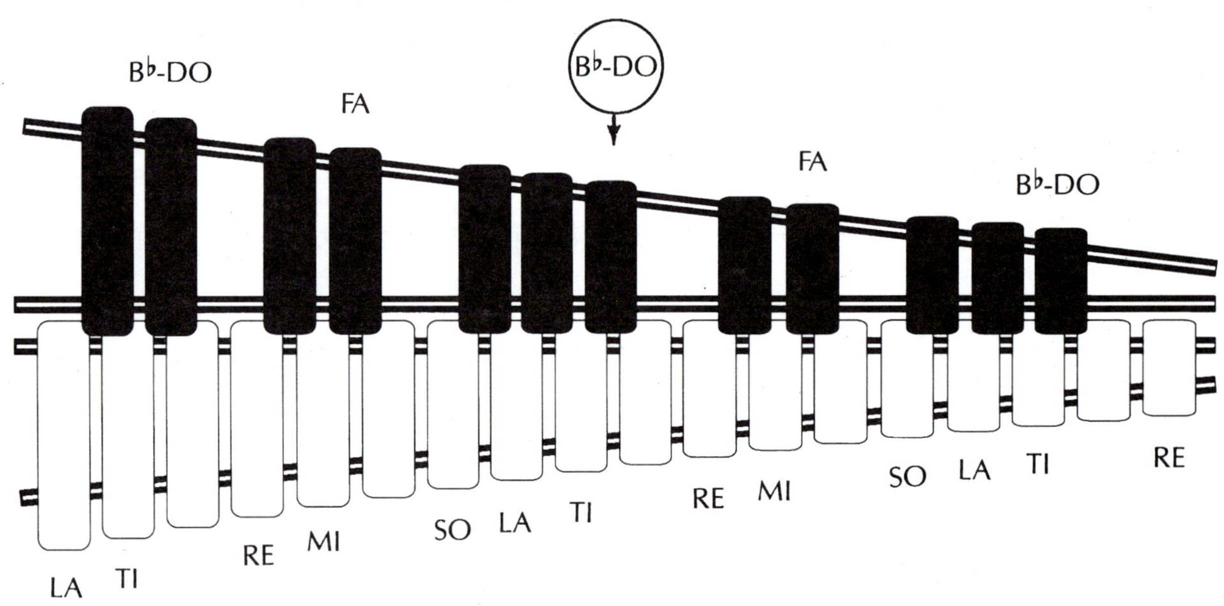

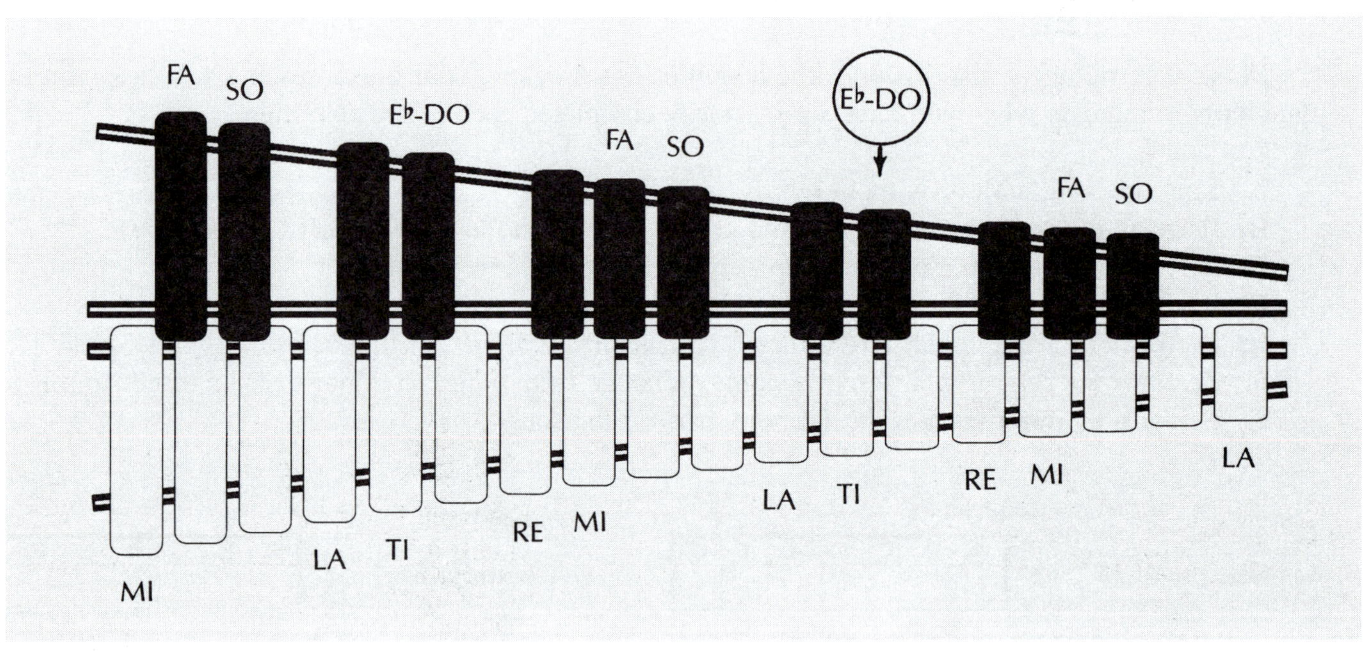